a Guide to Reading the Old Testament

Part Two

The Stage Is Set

Revised Edition

ACTA Foundation
4848 Clark Street
Chicago, Illinois 60640

NIHIL OBSTAT
   Thomas B. McDonough

IMPRIMATUR
   † Joseph Cardinal Bernardin
      Archbishop of Chicago
      January 30, 1986

Published by ACTA
4848 N. Clark St.
Chicago, Illinois 60640
(312) 271-1030

Library of Congress Catalogue No. 85-70360
ISBN No. 0-914070-22-3

Printed in the United States of America

INTRODUCTION

In recent years it has become increasingly apparent that familiarity with Sacred Scripture is a well-nigh indispensable part of the formation of modern apostles. The great work of building up the Body to the measure of the fullness of Christ, its Head, whether in the field of social action, or the liturgy, or education, etc., will be so much the more effective insofar as it draws on the wellsprings of the Bible for its inspiration.

The individual Christian, no matter what form his ministry may take, has a great need for a deep, mature faith as his mainstay. The word of God, studied and pondered in moments of recollection, can have a vital role in developing such a faith.

In a booklet like this it is impossible, of course, to do more than sketch the main features of Biblical literature. If it removes a few misunderstandings and shows the relevance of the message of some of the books of the Bible to our human situation today, the time and effort expended in its composition will have been eminently well spent.

This is the second of four booklets of eight lessons each. The booklets cover the whole sweep of the Bible from beginning to end. The first booklet traces the development of God's plan from its beginning with Abraham some 2,000 years before the birth of Christ up to 1,000 years later when Israel broke into two separate kingdoms. This booklet covers from then to the birth of Christ.

A word of sincere thanks to Daniel Lupton who wrote the original manuscript and to Russel Barta, Rev. John F. McConnell M.M., Rev. Roland Murphy O'Carm, and the Rev. Thomas McDonough who contributed suggestions for the original text. Rev. Edward Mehok and Rev. Gerard P. Weber updated the text.

The four books in this series

(Available in English and in Spanish)

A GUIDE TO READING THE OLD TESTAMENT
   PART ONE: GOD BEGINS
   PART TWO: THE STAGE IS SET

A GUIDE TO READING THE NEW TESTAMENT
   PART ONE: THE MYSTERY OF JESUS
   PART TWO: THE WHOLE CHRIST

ACTA (ADULT CATECHETICAL TEACHING AIDS) is a not-for-profit organization. Its purpose is to assist in the teaching of the Catholic Faith through the preparation of materials, such as texts, films, and recordings.

CONTENTS

LESSON ONE

Royal harpist

"Sing to the Lord"

BEFORE YOU OPEN YOUR BIBLE

The Bible in miniature: It has been said that if the Old Testament had been lost in some great disaster, most of it could be recreated if the BOOK OF PSALMS had been preserved. This collection of religious poetry, containing some 150 poems in all, is called the *Psalter*. The name is taken from the Greek word for harp or lyre which was used to accompany the singers when the psalms were used in the Temple worship. They were not written at one time or by a single author, although the whole collection is dedicated to David because of his fame as a poet and singer of psalms.

The drama of salvation: In the Psalter we have the fruit of centuries of prayer and meditation upon the great saving events of God's activity in the history of his people. This history might be imagined as a four-act play. The cast of characters comprises God, the Hebrews (both the individual Jew and the nation as a whole), and the "wicked," or God's enemies. In a sense, then, our four-act play is a thumbnail sketch of the action of the whole Old Testament. It is this panorama of salvation-history which forms the context in which we must read and pray the psalms.

The *First Act* might be entitled "Election and Covenant." As the curtain rises, God chooses a single people to be his people in a special, unique manner. He pledges them his *fidelity,* while they in turn vow *obedience* to God.

The *Second Act* could be called "The Covenant is Broken." Here we see the dreary record of national and personal *infidelity* to God, as it unfolds across the pages of Israel's history.

In the *Third Act,* "God is Angry," we find *punishment* in the form of (a) natural catastrophes; (b) the wicked, as God's instruments, oppressing the faithless children; and (c) God himself, abandoning his chosen ones, becoming the "hidden God." Then the nation responds with *repentance.*

Act Four, the last act, is entitled "God is Faithful." Here we behold the joyous climax of forgiveness and *restoration* of God's people to friendship. The psalms, then, are a reliving of the great drama of Sacred History by the community and the individual.

NOW OPEN YOUR BIBLE AND READ:

(NOTE: it is suggested that the reader study each of the psalms twice. The first reading should look solely to the beauty of the psalm as poetry. The second reading should be done in conjunction with the notes for each psalm found in the "Behind the Words" section).

    I. Hymns of Praise:
       PSALM 8
       PSALM 29
       PSALM 122

    II. Petitions:
      A. of the nation
       PSALM 60
       PSALM 80
       PSALM 137

      B. of the individual
       PSALM 18
       PSALM 22

A Reminder: The reader should bear in mind that the two outstanding features of Hebrew poetry are the *concreteness* of the images and the *parallelism* of the development of ideas.

Concreteness: The Hebrew mind was not given to forming abstract ideas as was the Greek. This psychological fact helps us to understand why the Hebrews never developed a true philosophy. To a Jew a man did not have a "soul," he contained "God's breath," "the breath of life." A good man was not one who possessed "goodness" but one who was deaf to the advice of the wicked, avoided their company, delighted in God's Law, etc. (PSALM 1)

Parallelism: Psalm 2 provides a good example of what we have called the parallelism of Hebrew poetry. Notice how the second half of each verse repeats the idea of the first half in different words.

"Why do the nations rage//and the peoples utter folly?

The kings of the earth rise up//and the princes conspire together against the LORD and his annointed:

'Let us break their fetters//and cast their bonds from us!' "

behind the words

The poems of the Psalter fall, more or less exactly, into four classes: hymns, petitions, didactic or instructional psalms, and prophetic psalms.

THE HYMNS OF PRAISE

The hymns all follow with greater or lesser fidelity the following plan:

Part 1—An *appeal* to praise the Lord. This appeal is addressed to the just, the nation of Israel, the community of nations, or even to the psalmist himself.

Part 2—*Motives* for praising God. These may be born of joy or reverent awe in the face of God's activity in nature or human history.

Part 3—*Conclusion*. A renewed appeal to praise the Lord. The psalms of this type are usually poetic reflections on the themes elaborated in GENESIS, ch.1; ISAIAH, ch.10; JOB, ch.36; or SIRACH, ch.42. It might be well worthwhile to read over these chapters before reading the three hymns we have selected for study.

Psalm 8—The majesty of God and the dignity of man: The theme of this psalm is the marvel of God's choice of human beings to be the chief revelation of himself and his representative on earth. It finds striking confirmation in the Incarnation of Christ. The words of the author of the EPISTLE TO THE HEBREWS, ch.2:5-11, form an excellent commentary on this psalm.

Psalm 29—God's majesty in the storm: The violent storms of the Palestinian coast were often used by the psalmists as an image of the divine power and majesty. It would seem that the occasion for this poem was a storm that came up over the seacoast and moved north over the heights of Lebanon, dissipating its fury over the Wilderness of Cades. In thus avoiding the territory of Israel and "attacking" the lands of her enemies, the psalmist saw in the storm an image of God's favor to his people.

Psalm 122—The pilgrim's greeting to Jerusalem:
One of the most striking features of ancient Jewish piety was love for the Holy City, Jerusalem. St. Paul sees Jerusalem as a symbol of the unity of God's people and a figure of the Church, (THE EPISTLE TO THE EPHESIANS, ch.2:20-22.) This psalm is best understood as the meditation of a pilgrim who, having returned to the quiet of his home, reflects upon the stirring memories of his pilgrimage. In later times it became one of the traditional pilgrim hymns sung as the groups making a pilgrimage to Jerusalem entered the Holy City.

THE PETITIONS

The psalms of petition or "asking" psalms make up the largest and most important element in the Psalter.

Psalm 60—Prayer of the nation in defeat: This psalm is a prayer of the whole nation, born of the tragic catastrophe of 586 B.C. (The Exile), when the nation was conquered by the Babylonians and the people transported to new homes in Babylon. This psalm most probably found a place in the official worship of the Temple on days of national mourning and the anniversary of the destruction of the Temple.

Psalm 80—Prayer for the restoration of Israel:
The image of the vine, representing God's people, is found

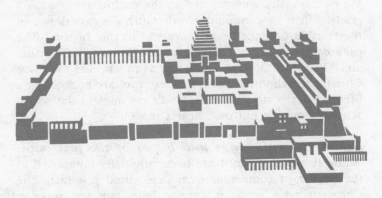

Temple of Solomon

again and again in the Bible. It is used here by the psalmist to depict the plight of prostrate Israel. This image occurs frequently in the writings of the prophets, (HOSEA, ch.10 and ISAIAH, ch.5) as well as in the Gospels, (MATTHEW, ch.20 and JOHN, ch.15).

Psalm 137—Prayer of the exile: The picture of the homesick exile sitting by the banks of a foreign river after a hard day's work and filled with a terrible longing is immediately winning. The violent and savage cry of vengeance of the psalm's conclusion, however, is quite shocking. But we must bear in mind that in the psalmist's day implacable hatred of Israel's enemies was the correlative of intense love for her. The practice he describes in the last line was commonplace in the warfare of the day.

The Psalter has been called the prayerbook of the Church. Down through the centuries, it has formed the backbone of the official prayers of the Church's worship. Yet we may wonder at this. How can these ancient prayers, wedded to a national history long past and filled with strange and, to our ears, savage expressions, rest naturally on the tongue of the Christian at prayer? How can a Christian say "Happy the man who shall seize and smash your little ones against the rock!"?

First, we must always keep in mind that the drama of the Jews is not a narrow, national history, *it is the drama of salvation* which lives on in the life of Christ, the life of his Church, and in the life of the individual Christian. Seen in this light the admittedly violent curses and barbaric raving occasionally encountered in the psalms are seen as a poetic effort to communicate the author's experience of the terrible urgency he encountered in that history. The psalmist was involved in a desperate life and death struggle. This sense of urgency is just as much ours as it was Christ's and the psalmist's. For we, too, are engaged in a life and death struggle with God's enemies in the world around us and in our own hearts as well.

Psalm 22—Sufferings and hopes of the just man: While this psalm may have been originally composed as the prayer of some unknown persecuted just man, the Christian who reads it cannot help but see amazing parallels between many of its verses and episodes in the Passion of Christ. It is frequently used by the Evangelists in the Passion narratives and Our Lord himself prayed its first line on the Cross.

Psalm 23—The good shepherd: Without doubt this is the most famous of all the psalms. EPHESIANS, ch.3:17-19, and ROMANS, ch.8:35-39 comprise a beautiful commentary on this psalm. Note that the psalm is really two different pictures. Lines one to four show God's loving care under the image of a shepherd's solicitous care for his sheep. Lines five to six present God under the figure of a typical oriental host consumed with the proverbial Middle Eastern anxiety to make his guest feel at home.

Psalm 51—A plea for forgiveness: The date and origin of this poem are not completely certain. Some scholars assign it to David himself, while others are inclined to place its composition after the Exile. In either case, the sentiments of this beautiful prayer are most fitting on the lips of David, the man "after God's own heart." For the Christian, it is a well-nigh perfect Act of Contrition.

Psalm 130—Out of the depths: This psalm is the famous "De Profundis." It is a prayer of penitence, but more than anything a hymn of humility and confidence in the merciful love of God.

THE DIDACTIC OR "INSTRUCTIONAL" PSALMS

The wise men of Israel made extensive use of the psalm-form to teach the people the "ways of the Lord." The themes of these psalms might be termed "pensive" or "reflective."

Psalm 78—A meditation upon the God who acts in human history: During the period of great trial for the nation, probably during the time after the return from exile, the psalmist drew consolation from God's "mighty deeds" for Israel in the past and saw in them a promise for the future.

13

Psalm 127—On the necessity for abandonment to God's providence: The psalmist has a double lesson for his hearers. First, that a person's labor is vain unless blessed by God. Secondly, his blessings come to those whom he loves, though they may not have looked for them.

THE PROPHETIC PSALMS

These psalms bear witness to the keen awareness of the Jews that their hopes were not centered solely on contemporary events but upon the "promises" of God to be fulfilled in a glorious future.

Psalm 110—The priestly office of the Messiah to come: The reading of ch.7 of the EPISTLE TO THE HEBREWS is warmly recommended to the reader for an elaboration of the theme of this psalm.

Psalm 126—Song of the return from exile: The psalmist uses the occasion of the return of Israel from exile in Babylon as a foreshadowing of the beginnings of the Messianic Age to come.

the unity of the two testaments

The psalm as a form of prayer was common throughout the history of Israel. We find several examples of psalm-prayers in the Gospels, (the *Magnificat*—LUKE, ch.1:46-55, the *Benedictus*—LUKE, ch.1:68-79, and the *Nunc Dimittis* —LUKE, ch.2:29-32.)

But, as we have already said, since the Psalms are the Old Testament set to prayer there is hardly a page of the New Testament which does not contain some allusion or direct quotation from the psalms.

bible and church

The Church uses the psalms extensively in her official prayer life. They are recited by priests and religious as a major part of their daily Divine Office. A psalm is used as a response to the first reading at the celebration of the

Eucharist. Verses from the psalms are used at other places in the Mass. By this extensive use the Church reminds us that we are the People of God today and that our lives are also a drama of election, infidelity, punishment, and restoration.

> *"The fact that the prayer of Israel has become, as if spontaneously and effortlessly, the prayer of the Church, simply witnesses to the continuity of Sacred History which the whole Bible ought to help us to grasp. . . . In this way when we come to the end of the Old Covenant, everything is ready to welcome the new. But, inversely, in order that its "good news," that is to say its gospel, be received, there must be hearts that are prepared, souls that are souls of desire, whose desire is that of the Spirit. It is the Old Testament that constitutes this preparation. It is the Psalms that translate this desire. They are, therefore, rightly the Christian prayer, because they are the prayer by which the Spirit too taught us to ask exactly what the Father wishes to give us by his Son."*
>
> Louis Bouyer

It is the Son who now offers these prayers with us, sharing the journey with us and inviting us to see everything in the light of the Gospel. The more we understand the human response in the past, the more we will want to make the divine response in the present.

doers of the word

The Church may make the psalms her prayerbook in order to accomplish in her children that attitude of expectation and desire for the "Good News" of Christ. But each of us must then make them a reality in his own life. The prayerbook of the Church must become our prayerbook as well.

One way of making the psalms our own is to use them frequently in our personal prayers. Take a little notebook and list your favorite psalms. You might want to classify them under such headings as "Night Prayers," "Morning Prayers," "Preparation for Confession," "Preparation for Communion," etc. There are also various prayerbooks available which make extensive use of the psalms. You may want to obtain one as a help to praying the psalms.

questions

1. What is the backdrop against which the Psalmists wrote?

_____

_____

2. Name the four phases of God's activity in the history of the Jews:

   A. _____

   B. _____

   C. _____

   D. _____

3. List the four general types of psalms found in the Psalter:

   A. _____

   B. _____

   C. _____

   D. _____

4. Were the psalms all written at one period in Israel's history by one poet?

_____

_____

5. What do we mean when we say that the BOOK OF PSALMS is the "Official Prayerbook of the Church"?

_____

_____

topics for discussion

1. How would you describe the attitude of the author of Psalm 8 towards God, humankind and the world?

2. Use the sentiments in Psalm 122 to compose a greeting you could use as you go into church on Sunday.

_____

_____

3. What does Psalm 60 tell you about God?

4. How would you evaluate the "self-conception" (i.e., the way in which the psalmist thinks of himself) in Psalms 18, 22, 51 and 130?

5. Knowing what you do about the immortality of the soul, how would you rewrite Psalm 39?

_____

_____

BACKGROUND

The Psalms as Prayers

When we use the psalms as prayers, it is of the utmost importance that we realize, as with all of Scripture, that these expressions of faith have emerged from many different periods in the development of God's people. There was a time when the God of the Israelites was thought of as one god among many, but more powerful than the others. And like the pagan dieties, Yahweh could be angry, vengeful, whimsical. He could be moved to change his mind if properly placated. He was an anthropomorphic God, created in our image and likeness. Therefore, he would go back on his word and break the covenant, inflicting suffering on his people, or call for unmerciful revenge on their enemies. He detests sinners and punishes them while rewarding the good in this life because there is only nothingness and darkness after death for everyone.

We often encounter ideas and attitudes that differ radically from our own Christ-given perspective. This contrast has often caused people to shy away from some of the psalms or, even more unfortunately, to prefer them as expressions that justify unloving reactions. Moreover, the complaint is sometimes heard that the different moods of the psalmist do not express "my feelings." Perhaps the first thing to remember is that these were the prayers of Jesus as he identified himself with humanity in its weakness (the need to grow) and in its power (the desire to grow).

So often, the psalmist begins in the pits of unhappiness, even despair, groaning with self-pity. Then the attitude is gradually transformed as God's goodness and blessings are remembered. Expressions of frustration and anger give way to a renewed faith and trust. While we may find many of the statements alien to our perspective, we are called to realize that this is where people have been in their thinking, indeed where some people are today, and perhaps where we find ourselves at times. We are a pilgrim people in need of change and growth through prayer.

These are *our* prayers, not just *my prayers,* and they call us to compassion, understanding, and patience toward others less gifted with vision or more burdened with sorrow. Prayer also leads to self-realization as we vocalize feelings that we recognize as our own, even though they are inconsistent with the way of Jesus. The purpose of all prayer is not to change God, but to change us. Perhaps this realization calls us to reexamine our own prayer formulas just as we must use the psalms with a new perspective. Our expressions of faith and need today should reflect our growing awareness of God as unchanging in his love, reaching out to us to save, not to avenge, lifting us up not by manipulation, but by grace.

We lift our hearts and minds to God so that we may grow in knowledge and love of our creator and savior. In the process, he is our sanctifier, making us holy as he is holy, enabling us to love others and ourselves as he does. Hopefully, we learn to be less envious of the material things enjoyed by worldly people, less vengeful towards those caught in the web of sin, more willing to sing the songs of Yahweh's praise as we walk the streets of Babylon.

LESSON TWO

Assyrian officer

"Holy, Holy, Holy!"

BEFORE YOU OPEN YOUR BIBLE

In this lesson we will meet Isaiah, the prophet, who tells the faithless people of the South, the Kingdom of Judah, about God's holiness, and its very real consequences for man.

"The year that King Uzziah died": (ISAIAH, 6:1) The days of Isaiah (8th century B.C.) were evil times indeed. The bitterness of civil strife between the North (Israel) and South (Judah) in the 10th century B.C. had resulted in undying bitterness and hatred. This emnity divided the two kingdoms like a wall.

With each passing day of Isaiah's life the terrible military machine of Assyria, expanding her great empire in the 8th century B.C., rumbled closer to the two tiny Hebrew kingdoms. It seemed inevitable that little Israel and Judah would fall beneath the bloody wheels of the Assyrian war machine.

Like its neighbor to the north, Israel, the Kingdom of Judah was sick with the merciless oppression of its poor. False religions, with their savage practices of sacrificing innocent children to their blood-thirsty gods, had also made sexual depravity a religious act. As Isaiah preached on the temple steps, the smoke of the fires where children were burned alive in sacrifice to Moloch, the god of the Phoenicians, could be seen smudging God's sky in the very heart of the Holy City! It was a time of intrigue, where men abandoned God and looked to political alliances with undependable Egypt or with savage Assyria as the sole means of saving their country from national extinction. Men looked to make covenants with the powerful and mighty, forgetting their Covenant with the All-powerful and Almighty God!

The Plan of God: In Part One of *A Guide to Reading the Old Testament,* we took a bird's-eye view of the beginnings and first stages of God's plan for the happiness of his people. This plan was to reach its fulfillment in Christ and his Mystical Body, the Church.

We have seen that many of the events which shaped this plan are not dead history but have a real importance right here and now. For we are the People of God, today! We are Abraham's children by faith. We are united in sharing the New Covenant as were the Israelites who shared in the Old Covenant. We know the dynamic force of God's Law in our lives as did the author of Deuteronomy. We are looking forward to entering the Promised Land of Heaven. God has said to us also, "You will be my people, and I will be your God."

Part two: Now we are embarking on the second phase, the period from the Exile (8th century B.C.) to the time of the Roman occupation (1st century B.C.), of God's activities in human history. One of the most striking features of the second stage of God's dealings with people is the growing refinement and deepening of their knowledge of God and their own place in God's plan. Up to now the preparation of God's people had been largely external. They had become a nation with a law and land of their own. Now the internal development of God's people was intensified. It was the privilege of the Prophets of God to carry Israel and the world a giant step forward along the road to a meeting with God.

God's messengers: In Part One of *A Guide to Reading the Old Testament,* we met the prophet Amos—he was God's courier to the Northern Kingdom, Israel. His message was, "Israel must reflect God's justice." Later in the 8th century B.C., Isaiah, steeped in the holiness of God, cried out, "God is just. God is holy. Israel must reflect this justice and holiness!"

NOW OPEN YOUR BIBLE AND READ:

> ISAIAH, ch.6 to 12—The Call of the Prophet and the "Immanual Prophecies"

> ISAIAH, ch.42 to 53—The Servant Songs

Some other beautiful passages you might like to read:

> ISAIAH, ch.5:1-7—The Song of the Vineyard
> ISAIAH, ch.11:1-16—The Golden Age
> ISAIAH, ch.12:1-6—The Song of Thanksgiving
> ISAIAH, ch.14:3-23—The Satire on Babylon

behind the words

An anthology: We might be tempted to call the Prophet's book, the "Portable Isaiah." For it was most probably assembled by disciples of the prophet some years after his death. There is little or no attempt to set down the sermons and poems in any kind of strict chronological order. The editor does not even attempt to give his collection a story thread upon which to hang the various selections. He seems to have included material written by other sacred writers during the Exile. He probably felt they belonged to the same tradition or school of thought which Isaiah had fathered or gave evidence of the fulfillment of Isaiah's warnings to the people of his day. The latter half of the present book is often called "Second Isaiah" (ch.40-66) as most of the material included here was probably composed after the prophet's death, during the Exile and after the Return.

Because the book is more of an anthology than anything else, we have selected a few of our favorite passages hoping they will whet your appetite for more. The BOOK OF THE PROPHET ISAIAH is a kind of smorgasbord where there is something to suit every taste.

23

Isaiah, the man: He was a member of the nobility. For this reason he had easy access to the king and high officials of the nation. He seems to have played the role of elder-statesman throughout most of his career. He was a keen observer of his times, and his deep insight into the awesome holiness of God did not cause him to divorce himself from life. His life was a perfect wedding of the mystic we meet in ch.6 enraptured with a vision of God's majesty and the politician discussing affairs of state with King Ahaz in ch.7. Even on merely practical grounds, his policy of neutrality and non-intervention in the struggle for control of the ancient world raging between Egypt and Assyria-Babylon may well have been the only course that could have saved the national integrity of Judah.

WRITE IN THE MARGIN OF YOUR BIBLE:

"The Call of the Prophet"—next to ISAIAH, ch.6:1

"The Emmanuel Prophecies"—next to ISAIAH, ch.7

"The Songs of the Suffering Servant"—next to ISAIAH, ch.42

understanding these selections

THE CALL OF THE PROPHET

The vision contained in ISAIAH, ch.6:1-13 sets the tone of the whole of Isaiah's mission. He was to be the great prophet of God's holiness. In the Old Testament, the idea of holiness meant to be *separated* from whatever is base and impure. Applied to God, it signified his complete *apartness* and distinction from the things he had created. In this context it is interesting to note that the term "phari-see" which we meet in the New Testament meant "the separated one." In this case it meant the Pharisee was separated from the common herd of the people, poor and ignorant of the Law, and thus free from any contamination from the people.

God stands completely above and apart from his creation: Yet this is *not* the whole story, for God's holiness is also active and makes demands upon people. For God is also holy because he *makes holy*. He wishes his creation to share his holiness. In Isaiah, then, we will meet the first faint outlines of the great mystery of Grace and Redemption. God wishes creation to *share* in his holiness, and man to share his own divine life!

ISAIAH, ch.6:1—It is interesting to find that the vision takes place in the Temple. Up to this time the appearance of God to men had taken place almost exclusively in dessert places. The picture which Isaiah paints is very similar to what one might have seen in the audience hall of some great Oriental potentate, with the monarch seated upon a winged throne.

ISAIAH, ch.6:5—You may wish to compare this more or less traditional attitude which Isaiah expresses with Gideon's vision in JUDGES, ch.6:22-24 and that of Manoah in JUDGES, ch.13:9-23.

ISAIAH, ch.6:8-13—Here we find a perfect description of the prophetic vocation. We often think of the prophet as one who foretells the future. But this point is only incidental to the true prophetic vocation. The word "prophet" really means "one who speaks for another." The prophet was to speak to the king and people. He was to speak for God. He was the national conscience. Sometimes in his role of public conscience it might be necessary to point out the future results of present conduct, but this was not always necessary, or a primary feature of the prophet's work.

ISAIAH, ch.6:9-13—At first we might be surprised at the description given of Isaiah's life work. But God is describing to the prophet the reception which his message will actually receive from his human audience. The word of God demands a response from those who hear it. The whole of the Bible can be called a dialogue between God and the human race. Sometimes people turn a deaf ear to God's word, but this is also a response.

THE EMMANUAL PROPHECIES

In ISAIAH, ch.7 to ch.11, we find the predictions of the Messiah to come.

Historical background: (ISAIAH, ch.7:1-25) Throughout this period (742-725 B.C.), Assyria was an ever-growing menace to the independence of the petty princelings of Palestine and Syria. Having secured the unreliable backing of Egypt, a mere shell of the powerful Egyptian empire of an earlier day, three of these little kingdoms formed a coalition under the leadership of the city of Damascus. King Ahaz of Judah refused to join the league. This was disastrous to the plans of the league because Judah was the overland link with Egypt in case they should need military assistance from the South. The only thing for the coalition to do was to march on Judah, dethrone Ahaz, and put one of their own men in his place. At the time of this meeting of Ahaz and Isaiah, word had reached the capital that the coalition was marching against it. It was probably on a tour of inspection of the fortifications that the monarch met the prophet (II KINGS, ch.16:1-20).

Who was Emmanuel? In ISAIAH, ch.7:14-15 the prophet introduces us to a new character in biblical drama, Emmanuel. The name in Hebrew means "God with us." The scholars have come up with various explanations of this passage. Some have claimed that Emmanuel refers to a son to be born to Ahaz himself, others to Isaiah's son, and still others to the Messiah to come. This last is the traditional explanation given down through the centuries by both Judaism and Christianity. It may well be that Isaiah was referring to some contemporary event, as this would seem to be necessary if the king was to have a "sign" in his own lifetime. But the light of faith shows us that this contemporary event was to be merely a first step to the complete and definitive fulfillment in the virgin-birth of Christ.

THE SERVANT SONGS

The poems contained in ISAIAH, ch.42 to ch.53 are called "The Servant Songs" because they are about another mysterious person only identified as "My Servant."

Song #1 (ISAIAH, ch.42:1-4) God presents his servant to the heavenly court. Here we find a description of the servant's mission. He is to be the patient teacher of the true faith to all mankind. This song forms an interesting back-

26

drop to the Baptism of Jesus in the Jordan River (MARK, ch.1:9-13).

Song #2 (ISAIAH, ch.49:1-6)   Here the servant speaks out to the whole world. It is interesting to note that like Christ, the servant's mission is first to the "lost sheep of the House of Israel," but apparently (ISAIAH, 49:6) he will leave this work incomplete and turn to the nations.

Song #3 (ISAIAH, ch.50:4-9)   This might well be called the servant's Gethsemane. But even in the face of suffering he does not lose confidence in the fulfillment of his mission.

Song #4 (ISAIAH, ch.52:13 to ch.53:12)   This is by common consent the most important of the songs. It forms a striking portrait of the "Man of Sorrow."

Who is the servant?   The writings of the scholars read almost like a detective story as they try to piece together from the text an identification of the servant. The interpretation given it by Jewish scholars has been to identify the servant either with the messiah to come, with the nation itself, or with the faithful few in every generation. Christian scholars were unanimous in identifying the servant with Christ until the beginning of the 18th century. Today they are divided upon whether it refers *only* to Christ, but many would probably agree that the songs have definite messianic features. Jesus chose to fulfill this ideal of Sacred Scripture in his own person, and the Church under the guidance of the Holy Spirit has always seen in these passages a remarkable prophetic vision of the mission, passion and death of our Lord.

unity of the two testaments

The BOOK OF THE PROPHET ISAIAH has often been called a pre-Christian Gospel. Certainly few other books of the Old Testament are quoted as frequently by the Evangelists. And where Isaiah is not directly quoted, the Gospels will often allude to him. Just as St. Paul is called The Apostle, and St. Thomas Aquinas, the Theologian, Isaiah is well-termed the Prophet. If your Bible contains marginal cross references, notice how frequently you will find references to passages of Isaiah as you page through the Gospels.

bible and church

Without doubt, the words of Isaiah dominate Advent, the time when the Church prepares for the coming of the Lord. On the Sundays of Advent, the first reading in Cycles A and B is from Isaiah, except for the fourth Sunday in Cycle B, and the first readings from all three Christmas Masses are taken from his prophecies.

His Suffering Servant Song is used as the first reading on Palm Sunday and on Good Friday, and his beautiful words about the role of the Messiah—to bring glad tidings to the lowly, to heal the brokenhearted, to free captives, and to comfort those who mourn—are read at the Mass for blessing the Holy Chrism on Holy Thursday. In fact, more selections from him are read at the liturgy than from any other book of the Old Testament.

doers of the word

Chapter 6 of Isaiah paints a picture of the call of a man who felt he was unworthy to be God's messenger. When he heard the call of God he cried out, "Woe is me, I am doomed. For I am a man of unclean lips . . ." (ISAIAH, 6:5) The Lord sent an angel holding a burning ember and touched his lips to purify them. Then when the Lord asked, "Whom shall I send?" Isaiah answered, "Here I am, send me!" (ISAIAH, 6:8) Each of us is called to carry the Lord's message to the people with whom we live. Most of the time we are uncomfortable in this role. We do not feel we know enough. We feel unworthy, even sinful. We are afraid we will say the wrong thing or get into an argument. We have many reasons for keeping silent. It might be helpful to memorize the short prayer the priest says before he proclaims the Gospel at Mass: "Almighty God, cleanse my heart and my lips that I may worthily proclaim your Gospel." We could say this prayer if we are called upon to read at Mass, but more importantly we could say it when we feel called on to speak for God and about God. This call comes more often than we think. When it does come, we need to answer it as Isaiah did. We need our hearts and lips to be purified of all pride or contentiousness.

questions

1. How does the second period in the development of God's plan differ from the first period?

   _____

   _____

2. What do we mean when we say that Isaiah is the prophet of God's Holiness?

   _____

   _____

3. Why is it true to say that a prophet is not mainly one who foretells the future?

   _____

   _____

4. Why was Isaiah able to see the king so easily?

   _____

   _____

5. Is there any similarity between the political situation of Isaiah's day and our own? Explain.

   _____

   _____

   _____

29

topics for discussion

1. What do you think is the most characteristic feature of Isaiah's message? What can we learn from this feature that could influence our own religious attitude?

2. Recall a time when you may have felt a call to speak out about God or Jesus. How did the call come? How did you feel? What did you do?

3. How do you account for Ahaz's attitude in ISAIAH, ch.7:14-16?

4. When you hear the words "Emmanuel" or "Saviour," what image comes to your mind? What do these words mean to you in your own life?

Group Discussion of the Bible

The study and reflection on the text of the Bible by the individual is fundamental to developing those insights which deepen and vitalize our Christian faith. But the study and discussion of Sacred Scripture by a group can add much to our understanding of God's word.

Both approaches are complementary. Both strive to achieve the same goal. We may describe this goal as the understanding of what the Sacred Writer intends to communicate, the circumstances in which he wrote, and the meaning of his message for the lives of each of us.

We have said that individual study and group discussion are complementary. Group discussion with a competent leader achieves the pooling of the insights gained through individual study and provides a critical examination of those insights to test their validity. Further, the interaction of group discussion will often open up new insights of which the individuals comprising the group were previously unaware.

The serious reader of the Bible is searching for a personal understanding of God's dealings with us and the response these acts of God demand of us. Certainly no Christian is unfamiliar with the promise of Christ, "Where two or more are gathered together in my name, there am I in the midst of them." In what better way then can the individual Christian develop the "evangelical introspection" of which we have been speaking than through group discussion.

Of course, when we speak of group discussion we do not mean a mere "bull session" which often is merely a pooling of ignorance or misinformation. Each individual must be willing to prepare by carefully pre-reading the Scripture assigned in the lesson and the background and commentary found in the *Guide* or some other source.

The members of the group should bear in mind that they are there to discuss the *Bible* and not to use the Sacred Text as a springboard to discussion of some irrelevant or only tenuously related topic.

Every good group discussion of the Bible will include the following points although, it should be noted, not necessarily in the order listed here.

1. The leader should remind the group of the objectives of group discussion of the Bible.

2. The members should report on the results of their individual study using the questions given in the lesson as a guide.

3. The group should analyze particularly significant scriptural passages.

4. The group should discuss the various conclusions reached by the individuals and compare and evaluate them in terms of the Biblical Text and the context of our Catholic Faith.

5. The leader should formulate whatever common agreement has been reached, and point up areas where problems remain for future study or consultation.

6. Readings and questions for the next session should be assigned.

LESSON THREE

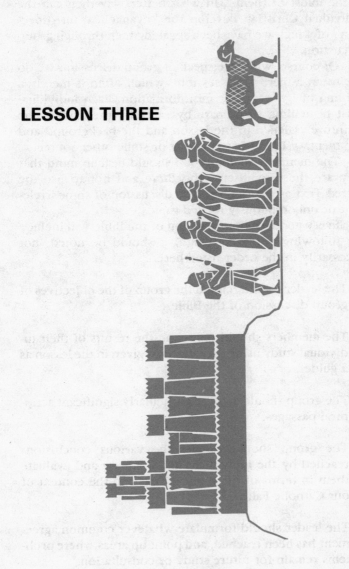

Exiles being led into captivity
(from the palace of Tiglath-Pileser)

"Behold the Day"

BEFORE YOU OPEN YOUR BIBLE

At each crisis in sacred history the Lord would raise up a man after his own heart. Just such a crisis arose with the conquest of Judah by Babylon. It marked a turning point in the history of God's people. The period of exile (6th century B.C.) put an end to the political life of the nation. God's promises to Abraham had been, up to now, interpreted mainly in a material sense. Now they were gradually seen in a new, a spiritual, light! This gradual change in the understanding of God's promises to Abraham was due, in no small measure, to the prophet Ezekiel. That Israel was now to see herself more and more as having a spiritual mission of bringing the knowledge of the one true God to the whole world was, without doubt, the greatest result of the history of the second period of the Old Testament.

It was during the period of Exile, almost 70 years, that the nation made its greatest strides toward realizing the goal God had set for it. Owing to the intensity with which religious life developed at this time, especially in connection with the Temple worship, the people became more like a religious community than a nation.

NOW OPEN YOUR BIBLE AND READ:

From the BOOK OF EZEKIEL

"The Prophet's Call"—EZ., ch.2 and 3
"The Exile"—EZ., ch.6 and 7
"The Allegory of the Faithless Wife"—EZ., ch.16
"Punishment and Pardon"—EZ., ch.18
"The Death of Ezekiel's Wife"—EZ., ch.24:15-27
"Hope and Consolation"—EZ., ch.33 and 34
"The Restoration"—EZ., ch.36:16 to ch.37:14

(NOTE: One of the most beautiful sections of the BOOK OF EZEKIEL is ch.25-32. Ch.27, 28:1-19 and ch.31:1-18 are especially worthwhile.)

behind the words

Ezekiel the man: Ezekiel was the son of a Jerusalem priest named Buzi. Ezekiel's father had been priest before him serving in the great Temple of the Holy City. Throughout his ministry, Ezekiel, a fearless and dedicated man of God, was intensely concerned with the affairs of Jerusalem. He was an ardent patriot and, of all the prophets, the most favored with extraordinary mystical experiences.

This combination of mystic and man of affairs is a striking one. Because of his visions, psychic experiences, and acted-out prophecies, Ezekiel may seem a very strange, if not bizarre, figure to the modern reader. But Ezekiel was also a prophet, priest, teacher, theologian, poet and organizer. In all his various roles one thing is abundantly clear, however. He was a man of towering faith. To the prophet Ezekiel, only one thing mattered supremely—the glory of God!

The River Chebar: Ezekiel lived and prophesied among the Jewish exiles in Babylon. He was the prophet of the Displaced Person Camps during the period from 597 to 538 B.C. While Jeremiah the prophet remained in Judah to bear witness to the Lord amid the chaos and ruins, Ezekiel in exile had the task of whipping a tiny remnant of God's people into shape. It was this little band which would one day return to the Holy Land and rebuild the nation.

As you read the selections, you may be puzzled by the apparent contradictory attitudes of the book. The first section (ch.1 to ch.35) is markedly pessimistic, while the second part (ch.36 to ch.48) is joyously optimistic.

The problem resolves itself if you bear in mind that the Exile forms the background for these prophecies. The deportation to Babylon took place in three stages. The first two groups of exiles were mostly courtiers and skilled artisans. They were taken as political hostages against the loyalty of the folks at home. Ezekiel was a member of this band. At first, the exiles were rather optimistic. They thought that as soon as the Babylonians were reassured of Judah's continuing loyalty, the exiles would be going home again. Of course the exile had been inconvenient and often uncomfortable, but it would soon fade away like a bad dream. In answer to this optimistic mood, Ezekiel replied, "If you think things are going to get better, prepare yourselves for a shock, you haven't seen anything yet! Jerusalem, itself, shall be destroyed!"

In 587 B.C., his words were bitterly remembered when news reached Chebar in Babylon that a revolt in Judah had been crushed, King Zedekiah of Judah taken prisoner, and the Temple and city destroyed! As the last band of tattered exiles reached Babylon, the whole Jewish community sank into the blackest despair.

Once more Ezekiel stepped forward. This time to play a different role. Throughout the dreary years of waiting, his words would be the one ray of hope, the one source of confidence of a prostrate nation. His watchword, "God has not abandoned his people" was a rallying cry to flagging spirits. One day there would be a new Israel, a new Jerusalem, a New Temple, a New Covenant between God and his people.

WRITE IN THE MARGIN OF YOUR BIBLE:

"Causes of the Exile"—next to EZEKIEL, ch.4 (This section was probably written before the destruction of the Temple in 587 B.C.)

"Against Judah's Neighbors"—next to EZEKIEL, ch.25 (probably written during the actual seige of Jerusalem)

"Words of Hope"—next to EZEKIEL, ch.33 (probably written after the fall of Jerusalem)

"The New Jerusalem"—next to EZEKIEL, ch.40 (probably written a few years later)

understanding these selections

EZEKIEL, ch.4-24: The prophet repeatedly points out that the terrible punishments decreed against Judah have but one purpose—to proclaim to Israel and the nations the nature and plans of God, Lord of the whole earth.

Ezekiel is the first of the prophets to bring out fully that God is interested in the individual person. The ancient Israelites were so strongly aware of God's concern for the nation, that they were practically unaware of individual responsibility and direct personal relationship between an individual and God.

Some commentators think that the death of Ezekiel's wife, obviously greatly beloved by the prophet, so stunned him that he was unable to give vent to his grief in the usual wailing and lamentation. God forwarned him of the personal tragedy that he might understand another significance beyond his personal loss. Others feel that the whole thing is a symbolic description of the grief of the exiles at the fall of Jerusalem.

EZEKIEL, ch.33-40: The fall of Jerusalem is the turning point in Ezekiel's career. To mark this transition from prophet of doom to prophet of hope, his call and mission are stated once again.

The gentle pastoral view of the Return from Exile pictures the Redeemer not in terms of an awe-inspiring conqueror, but rather as a humble shepherd. This is another step forward in the gradual, progressive understanding of the Messiah's mission on the part of God's people.

Israel's destiny was to be a *holy* nation, not a conquering one. The purpose of God's judgments had been to show forth his holiness to the nations by cleansing his people, their land, and temple. In the height of their national pride, the Jews had looked forward to a "Day of the

36

Ishtar Gate of Babylon

Lord." But instead of a day of triumph, it was to be the day of their condemnation. Yet the prophet looked forward to still another "Day of the Lord," the final day when evil will once and for all suffer defeat. In Christ the "Day of the Lord" was inaugurated and it will only be completed when all the kingdoms of the earth become his kingdom and he their prince forever.

unity of the two testaments

The Good Shepherd: Christ's words in which he describes himself as the *Good Shepherd,* (GOSPEL OF ST. JOHN, ch.10:1-16), form a striking development of the shepherd theme found in ch.34 of the PROPHESY OF EZEKIEL. Jesus is the "great shepherd," (HEBREWS, ch.13:20) who sums up in himself the whole pastoral ministry. He has come to "gather God's flock."

The new Jerusalem: The prominence which Jerusalem enjoyed in the Old Testament passes with the coming of the Messiah, to the Church here on earth and the "heavenly Jerusalem" (EZEKIEL, ch.40 to ch.48) which will find realization at the end of time (REVELATION, ch.21:1 to ch.22:5).

The covenant of peace: Again and again in the Gospels and Epistles, we find references to the New Covenant between God and mankind inaugurated by Christ. In fact, the whole collection of the sacred writings of the Christian Church are called the "New Testament," which is the Greek expression for the Hebrew "New Covenant." It is called *new* for two reasons: first because Jesus has fulfilled the Old Covenant: and second, because through this Covenant, sealed with the blood of the Savior, the Christian already shares in God's kingdom where "all things will be made new" (REVELATION, ch.20:5-7)

bible and church

St. Augustine in one of his sermons referring to the Church as the New Jerusalem, commented:

> *"This city is therefore now being built. Stones are now being hewn from the mountains by the hands of the preachers of truth, and are being cut square, that they may be fitted into an everlasting structure. Many stones are still in the hands of the Workman; and they must not fall out of His hands, if they are to be well and truly built into the fabric of the temple. This then is that Jerusalem which is being built as a city; and her foundation is Christ."*

Unfortunately, many Christians are tempted to evaluate the success of building the New Jerusalem by the size of the buildings and the number of members in the community. This leads to a complacent comfort in the apparent blessings lavished on good people and to a false security and anonymity within that group. To the superficial observer this is assuredly the day of the Lord's favor. But to the prophet, the danger signals are evident and he calls us to be concerned about spiritual rather than material growth.

When the numbers of church-goers dwindles, and religious vocations decline, and the educational institutions close, and the old observances are ignored, we begin to feel threatened. But the prophet assures us that this is the day of the Lord, urging us to open ourselves to the refining and polishing of the Master Builder, who always supports us, so that we become not just part of an earthly structure, but solid members of the heavenly city of God.

doers of the word

The parish church is a concrete sign of God's presence among us, and a pledge of his promises to receive us into the Heavenly Jerusalem. For this reason we should take pride in making it beautiful and keeping it in good shape. It would be interesting to find out something of its history and especially something about the symbols, statues, and pictures which beautify it.

However, the church building is only that—a building. The parish is people, and these people by their openness to newcomers, their concern for the poor and oppressed, and their willingness to spread the Good News create the New Jerusalem in a particular neighborhood. By yourself, with your family, or with a friend, review exactly what you do to help make the parish a living community and how you hope your efforts will further the Kingdom of God. If you find that you do not do very much, honestly ask yourself, "Why?" Perhaps you will discover that your reasons for not participating are based on past experiences which you need to let go of or on unrealistic expectations of a very human community.

questions

1. Why was the Exile a great turning point in the religious development of the Jews?

2. Who was largely responsible for this change?

3. Where were the exiles taken?

4. What were the reasons for the prophet's early pessimism and later optimism?

5. What was the prophet's profession before his call?

topics for discussion

1. The hidden meaning of contemporary events was explained to the Hebrews by the prophets. Is there any counterpart to the office of prophet in the Church today? What do you know about a prophet's office? Compare EZ., ch.2 and 3 with ch.6 and 7.

2. Have we become so aware of personal responsibility that we tend to forget communal responsibility? How does one strike a happy balance? Compare EZ., ch.3:16-20 and EZ., ch.18.

3. Does the image of married love used by the prophet (EZ., ch.24:15-27) tell us anything about the patriot's love of country?

4. What did the prophet mean when he told the people God would give them a "new heart and a new spirit"? (EZ., ch.36:25-32; EZ., ch.18:13-32)

5. What do you think of the following?
   "One must get rid of the pious imagery which so readily creates the belief that belonging to a flock is an invitation to bleat like a gentle lambkin." (EZ., ch.33-34)

6. Read EZ., ch.16—This is the allegory of the faithless wife. How does it answer the following questions:
   A. Why does God punish?
   B. Why does he forgive?
   C. What is Israel's relation to the other nations?

Cherubim and Goddess from Damascus
(from the palace Hazael)

BACKGROUND

The Role of the Prophets

Today the popular meaning of the word "prophet" is someone who "foretells" the future. This is unfortunately misleading. The role of a prophet is rather one who "tells forth" in the name of the Lord. If God's people are over-confident and complacent, he warns them of their weakness and their need to REPENT. If they are discouraged, he assures them of God's loving concern and calls them to BELIEVE in his saving power. This has been the basic message of each prophet to every age.

The prophets are so convinced of Emmanuel—God's saving presence with his people—that they see new meaning in the distress of the times. The Suffering Servants of Yahweh endure the difficulties, not as meaningless pain, but as an opportunity for personal growth and community reshaping. The prophet is so convinced of this positive value that he envisions the ultimate results.

Eschatological discourse, a description of the day of the Lord for which the human heart yearns, becomes the final statement of faith and hope. It is an apocalyptic vision of blessed joy and peace which can only be described in human terms but with a divine truth which lies far beyond the worldly images. The human author can only describe in earthly terms what the Son of God will remind us is a kingdom not of this world.

The last chapters of Isaiah envision a new world in which the demands of justice will be satisfied and all peoples will come to recognize the glory of Yahweh. But the verses are strong with thought of revenge against the enemies. This attitude will be modified in later writers and finally in the teachings of Jesus who calls us to love our enemies.

Ezekiel's concluding chapters detail, not as a blueprint but as an elaborate expression of hope for perfection, the city and the temple of the future, the dwelling of God among his people. From this temple flow life-giving waters that transform all the waters of the earth, making them wholesome, giving healing and life and abundance. It is a dream of paradise regained, a never-ending springtime and harvest time, because as its name indicates, "Yahweh-is-there," and they have come to realize that he is everywhere and always and forever.

This poetry of human and divine aspiration will receive full-blown expression in the apocalyptic style of the authors of the BOOK OF DANIEL in the Hebrew Scriptures and the New Testament BOOK OF REVELATION.

LESSON FOUR

Winged bull
(Persian bas-relief)

> *"Each with one hand labored
> at the work and with the
> other held his weapon."*

A remnant shall return: Prophet had foretold it. Psalmist had sung of it. And now in the 6th century B.C. a pitiful handful of returned exiles were gathered in the once splendid city of David. God's People had returned! A fresh start, a new stage in God's plan for his people's happiness had begun! A further refinement in the understanding of the mission of God's people was underway.

Throughout the half-century of Exile, Jerusalem was largely uninhabited and in ruins. The fields were mostly untilled and the survivors had been greeted with apathy and even open hostility by those who had remained in Palestine during the Exile. These last were a mixture of Jews and Pagans with whom they had intermarried. This was hardly the glorious restoration the exiles had dreamed of in Babylon, and many gave in to despair.

The walls of Jerusalem: Nehemiah, the civil governor, labored valiantly to rebuild the walls of the city and establish a toehold for Israel in their former homeland.

Ezra, the priest, some years later labored with equal dedication to build a "Wall of Law" around the remnant of Israel. Behind this "Wall of Law" the Jews were to live a self-contained life. Political power was gone. The people had merely to look about them. The blackened ruins of the Holy City, the spying informers of the Persian Emperor, and their openly hostile neighbors all spelled an end to political prominence. But some of the leaders of the people, Ezra and Nehemiah in particular, were determined, at all cost, to keep the nation faithful to their spiritual mission of preserving the tiny flame of faith until the "Day of the Lord." On that day, God's plan would be fulfilled and his people triumphant.

NOW OPEN YOUR BIBLE AND READ:

NEHEMIAH, ch.2, 4 and 6
EZRA, ch.9 to ch.10:18

behind the words

The new Israel: It is with the return from Exile that we first encounter the word "Jew." This new word marks a new stage in the development of God's saving plan for his people's happiness. It was a time of preserving the faith handed down by their fathers and new growth towards a more spiritual faith. It was to this period that the customs and forms of worship familiar in New Testament times trace their origins. At this time the *scribes,* mostly laymen devoted to the study and application of the law, began their rise to prominence. Two new religious institutions, the council of elders or *Sanhedrin,* largely replacing the king as governing body of the People of God, and the various local *synagogues,* increasingly the center of religious teaching and worship, also date from this period. In the light of the New Testament condemnations of the "Scribes and Pharisees" we may be inclined to judge harshly the work of this age. But, while recognizing the abuses connected with these offices, we should not forget the role they were to play in preparing for the "fullness of time" when they would give place to the universality of Christ and his Church.

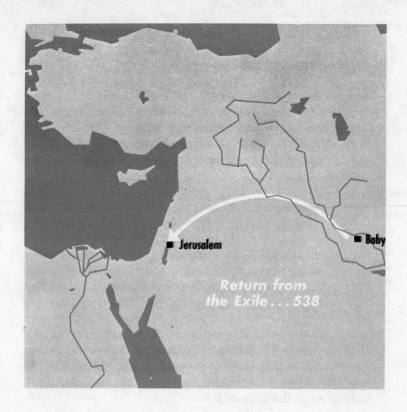

Jerusalem

Baby

Return from
the Exile . . . 538

WRITE IN THE MARGIN OF YOUR BIBLE:

"Let us build the walls of Jerusalem"—next to NEHE-
MIAH, ch.2

"The Mixed Marriage Problem"—next to EZRA,
ch.9-10

understanding these selections

"I set a date": (NEHEMIAH, ch.2:6)   Nehemiah was to ex-
ercise his office of Jewish governor for some 12 years. It is
interesting to note that Nehemiah carefully avoids any
mention of building fortifications other than the small
temple guard-post, as this would be sure to arouse the
suspicions of any Eastern monarch. That the Persian
emperor permitted the Jews to return to Palestine at all is a

47

striking example of the more liberal policies pursued by these monarchs in contrast to the crushing despotism of the Assyrians and Babylonians.

Sanballat and Tobiah: (NEHEMIAH, ch.2:10)   These two men were to head the opposition. Sanballat was the governor of Samaria, while Tobiah was the head of the wealthy Tobiad family. Both these men had a vested interest in seeing that no permanent restoration of Jews in Palestine came about.

The Samaritans: (NEHEMIAH, ch.2:20)   Compare this verse with EZRA, ch.4:1-6. The abhorrence which the strict and zealous leader of the new Israel felt for the surrounding people can be readily imagined. The Samaritans' offer to help in particular was brusquely rebuffed. The Samaritans were the people whom the Assyrians had planted in Northern Palestine to replace the deported Israelites (c. 721 B.C.). They had intermarried there with the remaining Israelites and adopted various observances of the Hebrew religion, mixing it with their native paganism. This refusal of help in rebuilding Jerusalem and the Temple was the origin of the feud between Jew and Samaritan lasting up to the time of Jesus.

A false friend: (NEHEMIAH, ch.6:10)   The walls were now finished and hence there was little danger of a successful military attack from without. Sanballat and Tobiah now embarked on a series of plots and intrigues. The particular scheme narrated here was an attempt to discredit Nehemiah in the eyes of the people. No layman was permitted to enter the inner sanctuary of the Temple.

The question of marriage with non-Jews: (EZRA, ch.9:1-15)   Throughout the history of God's people this had been a constant problem. The reader might be interested in looking up other pronouncements on this point (EXODUS, ch.34:15-16; DEUTERONOMY, ch.7:1-5; I KINGS, ch.11:7-13), which clearly show what a great danger to the faith intermarriage with neighboring pagans had always been.

A stern solution: (EZRA, ch.10) The harsh measures adopted were called for by the grave state of emergency then existing. The feeble band of returned exiles and luke-warm "people of the land" were extremely vulnerable to external influences. Understandably, Ezra felt that if marriage with neighboring pagan nationals continued, the little band of Jews would shortly be swallowed up and lost in the melting pot of the Middle East.

unity of the two testaments

There is a certain historical continuity between EZRA and NEHEMIAH and the Pharisees of the Gospels. The great concern which the two reformers showed for bringing about a restoration of Israel on the foundation of the Law had, to some degree, degenerated by the time of our Lord into a legalism which in the long run proved a serious danger to interior religion. But it would be a serious mistake to see their concern for a faithful carrying out of God's will for his people included in Our Lord's condemnation of the Pharisees. The Pharisees condemned by Jesus were the ignoble offspring of the noble and god-fearing generation of Ezra and Nehemiah.

bible and church

We have seen how Nehemiah and Ezra carried out the restoration of Israel on the foundation of fidelity to the Law of Moses. Origen who lived in Africa in the 3rd century A.D. shows the place which the Law takes in the life of the Christian. Echoing the statement of Jesus, "I have come not to destroy the Law but to fulfill it," he says:

> *"Jesus reads the Law to us when he explains to us the hidden things of the Law. For we, who belong to the Catholic Church, do not reject the Law of Moses, but we welcome it, provided it is Jesus who reads it to us. For, as he reads it to us we are able to lay hold of his understanding and interpretation. We must surely believe that St. Paul, who said, 'We have the mind of Christ, that we might know the things which are*

*given to us by God, which things also we speak,'
derived his understanding from that source. This was
true of the disciples on the road to Emmaus who said,
'Were not our hearts burning inside us as he talked to
us on the road and explained the Scriptures to us?'
(LK. 24:32). When beginning from the Law of Moses,
right on to the prophets, he read to them and un-
veiled all the passages which had reference to
himself."*

Christians today are still struggling to understand the
Commandments as Jesus understood them. Some people
are only comfortable when an authority tells them, "This
is what Jesus meant. This is what you must do or must not
do." Others do not want anyone telling them what to do.
They feel that "some inner voice" will tell them what is
right and wrong. Both are right and both are wrong. We
do need to follow the inner voice, our conscience, but that
conscience needs to be enlightened and guided by the
voice of Jesus in the Church.

doers of the word

Ezra and Nehemiah worked hard to rebuild a city which
had been destroyed. The Church has been shaken to its
foundations by the political, cultural, technological, and
religious changes of the past 25 years. These changes have
been felt on the parish level and rebuilding needs to be
done. We can look with nostalgia to the past or we can
take what we have and begin to rebuild. This rebuilding
will come about when the lay people willingly accept
various ministries in the parish, take an active part in set-
ting the direction of the parish and in implementing that
direction and when they gather in small groups to pray and
study together.

questions

1. Who were the two great reformers of the Return from Exile?

   A. _____

   B. _____

2. What new word was introduced into the Bible at this time?

   _____

3. What new advance did God's plan for man's happiness make in the 6th century B.C.?

   _____

   _____

4. What new professional class arose at this time?

   _____

   _____

5. What two new religious institutions appeared?

   A. _____

   B. _____

topics for discussion

1. Why would you say that Ezra and Nehemiah are models of faith?

2. In what ways do you see that you might imitate them?

3. What do you think of the rule laid down by Ezra in ch.9:12-15?

4. What do you think of the advisability of such a rule today?

5. What do you see as the difference between the way Ezra and Nehemiah went about restoring the Jews to fidelity to God?

6. What evidence do you see of these two approaches in the efforts to renew the Church after Vatican II?

BACKGROUND

The return from exile was a new start for God's people; the journey/pilgrimage of Abraham is repeated as they move from Babylon to Jerusalem. They, too, take the step of faith to establish the City of God, but with a different understanding of what that kingdom was to be. The old kingdom of Saul, David and Solomon had been destroyed; even the land had become divided as well as the people.

This remnant that returns, the new Israel, are the Yehudim, descendents of the people who formerly occupied the territory of Judah. They bring back a new name and also a new language (Aramaic becomes the language of daily life in Palestine) and new ways are introduced.

There emerges a new sense of community with priests and laity sharing responsibility as never before. They discovered that their God is not restricted by geographical and racial lines. He was with them in Babylon and worked through the pagans in their behalf (Cyrus in chapter one of EZRA and Artaxerxes in chapter two of NEHEMIAH are Yahweh's willing instruments). And now they could worship this omnipresent God not only in the Temple of Jerusalem, once a year, but in the synagogues of their own towns and, indeed, in their own homes, every week, every day, every moment. Their opportunities for religious education expanded on the local level as laymen became more knowledgeable in the sacred writings. It was a new era of lay participation, so similar to our own post-conciliar age. How essential it is for us to learn from both the success and failure of their efforts and to respond generously to the promptings of the Spirit in our journey/pilgrimage today.

LESSON FIVE

*"Ruth went and gleaned the ears of corn
after the reapers. . ." RUTH, ch.2:3
(figure from tomb of Meketre at Thebes)*

"A Light to the Gentiles"

BEFORE YOU OPEN YOUR BIBLE

The long years of captivity in Babylon had deeply impressed the exiles with the need of preserving a "remnant" to return to the Land of Promise. They refused at great sacrifice to be assimilated and disappear in the vast melting pot of Babylon. Steadfastly they maintained their national identity for the "return"!

A time of crisis: The return to Palestine after the Exile did not solve all the problems of God's people. It did not usher in a time of joyous prosperity and peace, as many had expected. Rather, it faced them with new challenges and conflicts.

A remnant shall return: In the BOOKS OF EZRA and NEHEMIAH we saw how the returned exiles, after nearly 70 years of struggle to keep from being snuffed out in the darkness of the Babylonian captivity, were now faced with the same problem on the sacred soil of Judah itself! The danger of absorption and gradual disappearance through intermarriage with the neighboring peoples was very real. The nation was fighting for its very life!

"Shall we again violate your Commandments?": Taken by itself, the prohibition against intermarriage decreed by Ezra could easily lead to a narrow and exclusive emphasis on racial purity as the touchstone of God's favor. "Do not presume to say in your hearts, 'We have Abraham for our father'; I tell you, God has power to raise up children to Abraham out of these very stones."

55

These words of John the Baptist were not the first protest against such legalism. Two little gems of the Old Testament, the BOOK OF RUTH and the BOOK OF JONAH were probably written during the period following Ezra's reforms. They provide a perfect balance to the tendency of some to push Ezra's directives beyond reasonable bounds and make them the sole content of religion for God's people. They point out that a legitimate fear of the dangers of intermarriage with pagans in general does *not* mean that the pagan is outside of God's providence (JONAH) or that in a particular case such a marriage cannot move the realization of God's plan forward (RUTH).

NOW OPEN YOUR BIBLE AND READ:

The BOOK OF RUTH, ch. 1 to 4
The BOOK OF JONAH, ch. 1 to 4

behind the words

A casual glance at these two books would seem to indicate that they are attempting to report straight history. But, thanks to the diligent work of modern scholarship, we now realize that we are reading a type of literature closer to our modern historical novel.

Ruth and Jonah compared: Both are stories with a point. The authors, writing after the period of the Exile, searched the ancient traditions of their people for historical figures through whom they could make an appeal for tempering the need of maintaining fidelity to the Covenant with the saving mission of Israel to the nations.

The author of RUTH chose to point out that the great king David was the descendant of a mixed marriage. Perhaps he also selected this ancestor of king David because of David's friendship with the Moabites of his day. (I SAMUEL, ch. 22:3)

The author of JONAH chose the prophet Jonah (II KINGS, ch. 14:25) to point out the universality of God's mercy. He contrasts the narrow self-righteousness of this "son of the Covenant" with the humble repentance of the gentile Assyrians.

"A Lesson in Fidelity"—next to RUTH, ch.1:15

"David, Descendant of a Gentile"—next to RUTH, ch.4:17-22

"Nineveh Repents"—next to JONAH, ch.3:4

"Jonah Embittered"—next to JONAH, ch.4:1

understanding these selections

The days of the judges: (RUTH, ch.1:1-5) The BOOK OF RUTH is set in the period of the Conquest of Canaan (c. 12th century B.C.). These were troublesome times. The land of Canaan was torn by war and strife. Famines were often the consequences of war. The fields were burned by marauding armies or left unsown while the men went off to do battle. Moab was the high country to the east of the Jordan River. It is interesting to note how careful and accurate our author is with his historical facts.

The plight of the widow: (RUTH, ch.1:8-14) In the economy of all the ancient peoples the lot of the widow was a difficult one. With no husband to be her champion and protector she was without position in the social order of the times. Needless to say, there was no opportunity for a single woman to earn her own way.

Ruth's loyalty and Naomi's destitution: (RUTH, ch.1:16-22) The beauty of Ruth's declaration of fidelity is unsurpassed in all literature and defies comment. Naomi's remark on her name is indicative of the importance which the Hebrews always attached to names. The ancient Jew would never agree with Shakespeare's "a rose by any other name would smell as sweet." They gave their children names at birth in the hope that their character would in some way be affected by the name they bore and would actually become worthy of the name they were given. Naomi's reference to evil as coming from God does not mean moral evil, that is sin, which is from man, but rather the natural calamities of death, earthquake, famine, etc.

The custom of Goel and Levirate: (RUTH, ch.3:1-13)
The word kinsman or next of kin in Hebrew is *Goel.* The
Goel had the right and duty to look out for the welfare of
his poor relations. He acted in God's stead as the Jews regard the Lord as the *Goel* of all Israelites. The custom
of Levirate marriage is recorded in DEUTERONOMY,
ch.25:9-10. Ruth's bold action was the customary pro-
cedure for a woman to propose marriage. Strictly speaking, Ruth, as an alien, had no right to benefit from these
customs of Israel.

The names of Jonah: (JONAH, ch.1:1) The meaning of
"Jonah" in Hebrew is "dove," while his father's name,
"Amittai," means "truth." The dove was used commonly
as a symbol for the Jewish people just as the early Christians used the symbol of the Fish. Thus, by God-given coin-
cidence we have "Israel, the son of Truth." *Nineveh* had
been the traditional major power in the near east. She thus
readily stands as a symbol of all Israel's enemies through
the ages. *Tarshish* is the Biblical name of Tartessus, a town
on the western coast of Spain on the very edge of the then
known world.

The hero of the story: (JONAH, ch.1:1) The title of the
book might lead us to believe that Jonah is the hero. But a
close reading shows clearly that the real hero is God. It is
God who constantly takes the initiative (JONAH, ch.1:1, 4,
17; ch.2:10; ch.3:1; ch.4:6, 7, 9). It is God who shows patience and mercy to all people, while Jonah is narrow and
vindictive!

The great fish: (JONAH, ch.1:17) The "great fish" is
used here as a symbol of the Exile brought on by the infidelity of Israel and designed to lead them through the
school of suffering and privation back to loving obedience
to God. The author of JONAH shows by this image that,
although the people returned to obedience, it was in many
cases a purely external conformity to the Law of God. In
this connection it is interesting to note that the name of
Nineveh, the archetype of Israel's enemies, means "town
of the fish."

unity of the two testaments

Ruth and Boaz are mentioned in the pages of MATTHEW and LUKE (MT., ch.1:5-6 and LK., ch.3:32-33) as the ancestors of the Redeemer. But, the whole BOOK OF RUTH is an interesting parallel of the Gospel events. For just as the chosen people failed in their mission of being the instrument of salvation for all the nations and separated themselves from the work of Redemption wrought by Christ, so also Naomi's next of kin was unwilling to be her champion or redeemer and another, Boaz, had to perform the function of bringing the gentile, Ruth, into the family of God.

Our Lord, himself, pointed out the pivotal message of the BOOK OF JONAH (LUKE, ch.11:29-32). Christ, who was greater than Jonah, invites all people into the Kingdom of his Father but upon the same terms as the BOOK OF JONAH, with a sincere and fundamental change of heart.

bible and church

The Roman Catholic Church is emerging from a time when all contact with non-Catholics was suspect, a time when mixed marriages were frowned upon and those involved considered unfortunate. The BOOK OF RUTH reminds us that many centuries ago, the author was telling God's People that outsiders have a great potential for good. The present ecumenical spirit in the Church is an indication that this message is penetrating the hearts and minds of God's People today. An ecumenical spirit does not mean that it makes no difference what one believes as long as one is seeking God, or that differences in beliefs and ideals are not important. But it does mean that we respect people who have a different religious tradition than we do. We are to seriously look at those traditions to see what is good in them, and how they can enhance our own belief system.

At one time we saw the world divided into two groups; those who wore the white hats (we Catholics who had the truth), and those who wore the black hats (the heretics or those who did not agree with us). Today we see that all people wear gray hats and that some beauty and truth can be found in all religions.

doers of the word

The responsibility of the Christian is a very grave one indeed, for we are charged with carrying God's message to Nineveh! "Go ye, therefore, and teach all nations." We might well take a moment to ask ourselves just how *effective* is our personal witness to the message of Christ and how wholehearted our cooperation in the world-wide mission of the Church. Perhaps we find ourselves more Jonah-Christians than Christians after the heart of St. Paul, who said, "Prayer of this kind is good, and God our Savior is pleased with it, for he wants all men to be saved and come to know the truth." (TIMOTHY, ch.2:3-4)

One thing we can do is pray for specific people that they may come to know Jesus. Secondly, we can be willing to talk about our own personal faith and relationship to Jesus. Religious discussions usually are to be avoided because they degenerate too easily into arguments about who is right or wrong. But the sharing of one's own experiences and feelings very often brings people together. Finally, we can volunteer to act as sponsors or helpers for the R.C.I.A. program in the parish, through which people are being inducted into the Church.

questions

1. What was the major concern of the pious Jew during the long years of exile?

_____

_____

2. What was the danger which the exiles faced upon their return to the Holy Land?

_____

_____

3. What modern type of literature is probably closest to the literary form used in composing the BOOKS of RUTH and JONAH?

_____

_____

4. What attitude among God's people were Ruth and Jonah designed in God's plan to modify?

_____

_____

topics for discussion

1. What image of marriage, widowhood and family life is conveyed in the pages of the BOOK OF RUTH?

2. Would you call the story of Ruth a "romance" in our modern sense of a tale of romantic love?

3. How do you explain Jonah's attitude?

4. Compare the BOOK OF JONAH with the Parable of the Prodigal Son (LUKE, ch.15:12-32).

5. What does God's way of dealing with Jonah tell us about human freedom?

LESSON SIX

Famine victim
(from Egyptian temple at Sakkarah)

"Job and His Friends"

In our study of the Old Testament we have seen again and again the wonderful manner of God's dealings with people. In one sense the plan of God for their happiness can be considered one vast process of moral and religious education. Like a good teacher, God always spoke in terms which his people could understand. He never demanded more of them than they were really capable of giving. We have already seen how this helps to explain God's apparent tolerance of the barbaric marriage customs and methods of warfare common to the peoples of ancient times.

But a good teacher is always anxious to stimulate his pupils to advance the frontiers of their knowledge. God too was constantly calling his people to greater and greater heights of knowledge and love of him and their fellow human beings.

The place of Job in God's plan: Pain and tragedy are, unhappily, a commonplace of human experience. In the earlier books of the Bible the communal solidarity of mankind was strongly emphasized. A person was blessed or cursed, in so far as the tribe or nation as a whole was faithful or fell away from God, (EXODUS, ch.20:5-6). Gradually individual responsibility came to greater prominence. This was largely the burden of the message of the prophets, particularly Jeremiah and Ezekiel, (EZEKIEL, ch.18:1-32). But both of these aspects of the problem of reward and punishment were understood solely in terms of material blessings or disasters. Further, there was a tendency on the part of many to interpret the relation between prosperity and virtue, or disaster and vice with an almost mathematical rigidity.

It is the great virtue of the BOOK OF JOB that it challenged this too pat explanation of God's governance of Creation. It advanced, at least negatively, the frontiers of revelation by introducing a figure who is clearly innocent and undeserving of punishment, and who stoutly denies the various traditional explanations of his so-called friends. JOB is not a book of "pat answers." Its function in God's plan was to question the accepted doctrine and break the ground for a much more profound insight into the problem of suffering. Job was to lay the groundwork for the great good news of the Gospels with their message of Redemptive Suffering, of victory in defeat.

NOW OPEN YOUR BIBLE AND READ:

The BOOK OF JOB, ch.1 to 7 and ch.38 to 42

behind the words

Author: The talented hand that produced the dramatic poem we call the BOOK OF JOB is unknown to us. Yet by a close scrutiny of his work biblical scholars have discovered a good deal about him. He was a native of Palestine, living some time after the return from exile. There is good reason to suppose he composed the book around the end of the 5th century B.C. He was a well-travelled man, being familiar with the religious traditions of the Egyptians and other Near Eastern peoples. No other Old Testament author except Ezekiel appears as learned. He was a keen observer of the world around him, and of a deeply compassionate nature.

Literary structure: The body of the BOOK OF JOB is a dramatic poem in dialogue form (ch.3 to ch.42:6). This poem is set in the frame of a much older prose narrative, (ch.1, 2 and ch.42:7-16). There is evidence for believing that this Prologue and Epilogue are a very ancient account of a traditional figure who lived prior to 1000 B.C. This personage may be identical with the Job mentioned in EZEKIEL ch.14:14 and 20. Taken by itself, the prose section gives a rather different solution to the problem of innocent suffering and was probably used by the author of our present work as a traditional introduction to his own highly untraditional and challenging poem.

WRITE IN THE MARGIN OF YOUR BIBLE:

> "Prologue"—next to JOB, ch.1:1
> "Job's Lament"—next to JOB, ch.3:2
> "The Great Debate"—next to JOB, ch.4:1
> "God Intervenes"—next to JOB, ch.38:1 to ch.42:6
> "Epilogue"—next to JOB, ch.42:7

understanding these selections

Job and the hereafter: (JOB, ch.3:13-23) The ancient Hebrews had very little knowledge of a person's fate after death. It is only in the very last books which were written shortly before the time of Christ (II MACCABEES and the BOOK OF WISDOM) that we find here and there a clearer picture of an eternal destiny. To the author of JOB the only thing which awaited a person at death was "Sheol." We might call "Sheol" an imaginative picture of nothing. It was one vast grave in which Death, the great leveller, placed all people sooner or later. The only thing the author knew for certain was that death ended life as we know it. What lay beyond it was hidden from his eyes. The answer to this question had to await a fuller revelation of God's plan for the happiness of the human race.

The prayer of Job: (JOB, ch.6:1-10) This outpouring of anguish and boldness is perhaps a little shocking to those of us more accustomed to the phrases of conventional prayerbooks. But we are told by the author that Job is a just man! It is, perhaps, because of his intimate relation with God that Job can speak so bluntly. These lines are somewhat reminiscent of the cry of Our Lord on the Cross, "My God, my God, why hast Thou forsaken me?"

The patience of Job: (JOB, ch.7:1-21)   Long before any of us ever turned to reading the Bible, we were no doubt familiar with Job as an outstanding model of patience in suffering. "He has the patience of Job" has become proverbial in our speech. This being the case, it is quite surprising to find Job voicing the sentiments we find in chapter 7! He seems to regard God (v.20 "O Watcher of Men") with hostility! Here we have the state of mind of one who knows the living and personal God but not his grace and love. In v.17, he seems to parody PSALM 8. In all this we have a striking example of the grass roots realism of Holy Scripture. Job must first be tried as by fire before he can come forth purified. This outburst is an expression of Job's torment. It is only after his confrontation with God that we meet the "patient" Job of ch.40:4-5.

Job and God: (JOB, ch.38 to ch.41)   Several important things occur in these climactic chapters. Job is humbled by the majesty and omnipotence of God. God's meeting with Job is itself seen to be an act of his gracious mercy, assuring him that he is not abandoned. The author accomplishes his main purpose, for the "friends" are rebuked, Job commended, and though God's righteousness in ruling the world is firmly maintained it is equally pointed out that people's misfortunes and sufferings cannot always be traced directly to their sins.

God and the world of nature: (JOB, ch.39)   This chapter is a strikingly imaginative description of various members of the animal kingdom. It is interesting to note that most of the animals described are the least companionable or useful to human beings. Perhaps this is an indirect correction of the excessively man-centered judgment of Job and his friends on God's activities. Compare this chapter with Our Lord's words in MATTHEW, ch.10:29.

God and the war horse: (JOB, ch.39:19)   This passage is one of the most famous descriptions of the horse in all literature. To the Hebrews the horse was what the atom bomb has become in our day, a really decisive weapon in war. The horse is taken here as a symbol of the great power which people can use but cannot create.

unity of the two testaments

Psychiatrists tell us that it is becoming increasingly clearer that the most basic drive of the human personality is the "drive for meaning." By this they mean the deep-seated need to understand the significance of the things which

Job's friends

happen in the course of one's life. The BOOK OF JOB poses this problem of "meaning" in one of its most acute forms. How often we have heard the tortured cry, "Why did this happen to me?" "What have I done to deserve this?" The full elaboration and solution of this problem did not come until God, himself, become human, showed the world the real "meaning" of innocent suffering on the hill of Calvary. God offered the human race the opportunity to transform temporal defeats into eternal victories through union with the suffering Christ. St. Paul comments on Christ, the second Job, in his letter to the ROMANS, ch.5:1-21 and St. James recommends Job as a model to the Christian in tribulation (LETTERS OF JAMES, ch.5:7-11).

bible and church

Throughout the ages the Church has not been any more successful than Job in explaining the ultimate reason for the suffering we experience in our own lives and see in the lives of people around us. But the Church does give us a way to make that suffering a bit more bearable and to use it for our spiritual growth. It holds up Jesus on the cross as a model of redemptive suffering borne with patience and acceptance. It calls upon us to join our sufferings with those of Jesus and to pray with him, "Not my will but thine be done."

Because the Church has not seen suffering as something good in itself, she has always tried to alleviate as much as she could. The care of widows, orphans, the poor and the imprisoned has been carried out in all ages. And today, when great attention is paid to the burden of mental suffering, Catholic Charity agencies supply counseling. Most of the extra collections taken up in parishes throughout the year are in one way or another connected with alleviating suffering in one form or another.

doers of the word

We should be amazed and embarrassed that so many centuries after the BOOK OF JOB was written and after the Gospel of Jesus was proclaimed, Christians so often sound like the "friends" of Job: "The poor deserve their condition because they are lazy and wasteful"; "the sick are justly punished for their sins and excesses." When catastrophe strikes certain places or people, it is gleefully proclaimed as fire and brimstone sent by an angry, vengeful God. The self-righteous Jonah still sits in the comfort of the castor-oil plant anxiously waiting for justice to be meted out to others.

The lack of human sympathy repels us. It can be a salutary reminder to us also. We must never allow ourselves to become complacent in the presence of the suffering of others. Human feeling, abundantly clear from the life of Christ himself, is perfectly compatible with holiness. Indeed, it is difficult to conceive of sanctity which would not include the beautifully human quality of compassion. We might well ask ourselves how we react to the tragedies of others. Do I visit the sick? How about my attendance at wakes and funerals? What is my attitude on such occasions? Do I try to "suffer with" the bereaved or is it merely an opportunity for social or business contacts?

questions

1. What purpose did the BOOK OF JOB serve in the working out of God's plan for people's happiness?

2. When was the BOOK OF JOB probably written?

3. How did the Jews of the 5th century B.C. picture the hereafter?

4. In what ways did God act like a good teacher in dealing with his people?

A. _____

B. _____

5. What kind of literary form is used in the BOOK OF JOB?

_____

_____

topics for discussion

1. In your own words describe God as he is pictured in the BOOK OF JOB. Is this picture the same or different than the one you have of God?

2. In what way do you see the BOOK OF JOB being modern in tone and story?

3. How does the author of the BOOK OF JOB solve the problem of innocent suffering? How do you solve it?

4. Read the BOOK OF WISDOM, ch.1 to 5, and the SECOND BOOK OF MACCABEES, ch.12:43-46. Do these passages add anything to the answer given by the author of Job?

5. Write your own dialogue between a modern Job and God. What would Job say today and how would God answer him?

Approximate Dates of Some of the Old Testament Writings

B.C.

12th Century Early songs, probably handed down by Oral Tradition

Song of Deborah and Barak (JUDGES, ch.5)

Song of Lamech (GENESIS, ch.4:23-24)

11th Century Song of Joshua (JOSHUA, ch.10:12), quoted from an ancient collection called The BOOK OF JOSHUA

Lament of David over Saul and Jonathan (II SAM. 1) quoted from the same collection

10th Century A few early psalms, e.g., PSALM 18

9th Century The Historical Books—SAMUEL and KINGS (Begun)

8th Century AMOS, HOSEA, MICAH, and ISAIAH, ch.1-39

7th Century BOOK OF DEUTERONOMY and JEREMIAH published under Josiah 621 B.C.

6th Century Period of the Exile 597-538 B.C.

Much editing of Early Books

Later PSALMS

EZEKIEL

5th Century Priestly writers at work, e.g., GENESIS, ch.1

4th Century EZRA, NEHEMIAH, BOOK OF JOB, ISAIAH 40-50, BOOKS OF RUTH and JONAH

3rd Century BOOK OF ECCLESIASTES

2nd Century BOOK OF DANIEL

Completion of PSALMS

LESSON SEVEN

Coins of the Maccabean period

"Let us go and make a treaty with the heathen."

"The Lord stirred up the spirit of Cyrus, King of Persia": From the time of Ezra and Nehemiah (c. 433 B.C.) the children of God had maintained their existence as a Persian province. We have already seen the renewed emphasis which was given to the Law and the Ritual of the Temple now that the nation no longer figured as even a minor political power on the stage of history. An apparently peaceful and uneventful stretch of more than 200 years follows.

"The whole earth was silent before him": But this peace was broken by a chain of outside events. Persia fell before a new force from the West. Alexander the Great added Palestine and Syria to the expanding Greek empire in 331 B.C. At his death a few years later, the Empire was divided among four of his generals, Ptolemy, Seleucus, Cassander and Lysimachus. At first Palestine fell to the Ptolemies who ruled the Egyptian section of Alexander's former Empire and were inclined to be tolerant of the Hebrew religion and way of life.

73

"A sinful shoot named Antiochus Epiphanes": In 198 B.C. Palestine was annexed to the Syrian segment of Alexander's Empire ruled by the Seleucids, descendants of General Seleucus. Their policy was one of enforced cultural and religious conformity. Everyone must become a Greek in language, culture, and religion, or else! A steady pressure was exerted on the reluctant elements among the Jews to become Greek in language, custom, religion and thought. This pressure exploded in 168 B.C. when Antiochus Epiphanes IV (Greek for "The Illustrious") desecrated the Temple at Jerusalem by introducing the worship of Zeus, the "father-god" of the many Greek gods and goddesses, into its holy precincts.

"Let everyone who is zealous for the Law come out after me!": This sacrilegious act was not taken lying down. A leading Jewish family, the Hasmoneans, better known to us by the nickname "Maccabees" which probably means "hammer" and was originally applied to their leader Judas, launched a revolt which was to rage for 30 years. For the first time since the days of the Divided Kingdom, some 500 years before, the Jews tasted the strong wine of military success and political importance.

The First Book of the Maccabees: Here we find an extemely vigorous account of the attempts of the Maccabees (Mattathias, the priest, and his five sons) to maintain the Jewish religion and way of life by force of arms.

It was written a little more than 100 years before the birth of Christ by a supporter of the Hasmoneans. The author was a resident of Jerusalem, an excellent historian, even by Western standards, and perhaps an eyewitness of many of the events he recounts.

His book covers the 40 years from the beginning of the revolt to the death of the last of the Maccabean brothers, Simon.

NOW OPEN YOUR BIBLE AND READ:

The FIRST BOOK OF MACCABEES, ch.1, 2, 3, 4, 6, 8, and 14

Antiochus IV Epiphanes
(from coin of the period)

behind the words

The link between old and new: The BOOK OF MAC-CABEES is an important link between Old and New Testament times. Together with the other late books of the Old Testament, it forms a prelude and background to the Gospels. In it we find already evident three outstanding characteristics of Judaism in the time of Christ. These characteristics are a profound consciousness of God's supremacy over his creation (I MC., ch.3:18-22), unbreakable attachment to the Temple and the Holy City (I MC., ch.4:36-60) and complete fidelity to the observance of the Law (I MC., ch.3:47-51).

These features of the religious life of the people were maintained at heroic cost. They were, however, gradually mixed with a certain rigidity and narrowness by some. This resulted in the blasphemous travesty of the service of God typified for all time by those Pharisees condemned by Christ in the Gospels.

Nevertheless, at the time of the Maccabees, these qualities helped to preserve and maintain the people in fidelity to God in the face of the very real danger of absorption by Greek religion.

"My kingdom is not of this world": The events of Maccabees also served a *negative* purpose in God's plan for man's happiness. After long struggle the Hasmoneans

75

succeeded in regaining national independence and even a certain political prominence.

Yet, the pious Jew was quick to learn the lesson that this was *not* the way in which the "blessings for all nations" promised by God to come through Abraham's descendants would be realized.

Political eminence would fade almost as quickly as it had arrived. In 63 B.C., the Roman general Pompey conquered Jerusalem and the world was no better a place and man no closer to friendship with God than in the year 168 B.C. when the fires of revolt had been enkindled.

Cast of characters: The historical figures mentioned are not only figures on the stage of history but are also, in a sense, larger than life. They are also players in the great *drama of ideas* which has fascinated man through the ages.

The war is not really between the Seleucids and the Hasmoneans, nor between the Jews and the Pagans, but it is rather between the observers of the Law and its adversaries, whether Jew or Greek.

Mattathias, father of the Maccabees, is a key figure in the great debate over the freedom and integrity of individual conscience in the face of the demands of the absolute state.

Alexander and Antiochus IV are, for the author, two examples of that overweening pride which is the complete inversion of a person's proper relation with God.

Judas, the soldier; *Jonathan,* the guerrilla leader; and *Simon,* the shrewd politician; are all in their various ways struggling to rescue their people from the first full-blown religious persecution in history.

WRITE IN THE MARGIN OF YOUR BIBLE:

"History Secular and Sacred"—next to I MC., ch.1

"Revolt of the Maccabees"—next to I MC., ch.2

"The Cleansing of the Temple"—next to I MC., ch.4:36-60

"The Roman Alliance"—next to I MC., ch.8

understanding these selections

Alexander the Great: (I MC., ch.1:1-10) This almost legendary figure of world history set out on his conquest of the world in 332 B.C. It is interesting to note in passing that the future ruler of the world was educated by Aristotle.

The "Greekizers": (I MC., ch.1:11-16) Not all the Jews were adamantly opposed to "the Greek Way." Not a few felt that the wiser course was to cooperate and curry favor, while a great many more had a real admiration for Greek ways and wanted to combine them with Hebraic culture to the improvement of both.

Persecution rages: (I MC., ch.1:26-29 and 38-42) These paragraphs are interesting examples of the poetical heights to which our ordinarily matter-of-fact historian occasionally rises. Compare these passages with PSALM 78, which was written around the same time as I MACCABEES, and note the similarity in spirit and style.

The "sons of Hammer": (I MC., ch.2:1-26) The family of the priest Mattathias came from the little town of Modin, about 15 miles northwest of Jerusalem. For the reference to Phineas in v.24, consult the BOOK OF NUMBERS, ch.25:7 and those following.

The pious ones: (I MC., ch.2:42) The "Hassidim" or Pious Ones were the forerunners of the Pharisees of the Gospel. They were a sect of pious Jews who rose to the occasion at this moment of religious peril by joining the Maccabees in revolt.

Feast of dedication: (I MC., ch.4:36-59) The event described was commemorated for future generations by the feast of Hannukah, or "lights." This feast is still celebrated by modern Jews and falls around Christmas time. For its mention in the New Testament, see JOHN, ch.10:22.

The elephant war: (I MC., ch.6:32-46) The juice of grapes and mulberries was used to suggest blood to the elephants and thus excite them to savagery in the ensuing battle.

Alliance with Rome: (I MC., ch.8:1-32) There is an old Arab saying, "Never let the camel get his nose under the tent. For if he does, soon he will be sleeping inside and you will be out in the cold." This observation was borne out in the case of the Roman alliance with the Jews. This treaty was the first step which inevitably led to the fall of Jerusalem to General Pompey in 63 B.C. Needless to say, Rome had no intention of supplying the military aid promised. The treaty was merely an attempt to embarrass the Seleucid monarchs by recognizing their rebellious province as a nation.

the unity of the two testaments

The BOOK OF THE MACCABEES is deeply concerned with one aspect of the problems of people's allegience to the state and to God. When some men asked Jesus whether or not it was lawful to give tribute to the emperor, they were trying to trap him into treason. But Jesus gave the sage answer of giving to Caesar what is Caesar's and to God what is God's (MATTHEW, ch.22:15-22). St. Paul also deals with the relationship of the Christian to the state in ROMANS, ch.13:1-8 and I THESSALONIANS, ch.3:1-13.

bible and church

Throughout history the Church has had to try to work out a way of living with the state. For centuries the kings and emperors felt that they were superior to the Church and they interfered in Church matters no end. Then in the early Middle Ages the Church felt it was superior to the state and the popes deposed kings and emperors. Since then there has been tension of all sorts. One of the great contributions of American theologians to Catholic thought has been the justification of separation of Church and state which we have in this country. For centuries theologians maintained that the state should serve the Church. As a result of the American experiment we now see that each has its own sphere and that each should keep to it. But even then there are problems, as when the bishops of the country speak out on injustice, nuclear arms or economics and when the state makes laws which are unjust. But when we look at other systems, our system is the best there is.

doers of the word

In our country, the Church has been wonderfully blessed. But, as we know, our fellow Christians throughout the world are not enjoying the same freedom. One most worthwhile result of reading the FIRST BOOK OF MACCABEES would be frequent remembrance in your prayers of the "Church of Silence" undergoing the terrible "persecution-harvest" in many countries today.

questions

1. What were the two major concerns of the Jewish community during the peaceful period following the Restoration under Ezra and Nehemiah?

   A. _____

   B. _____

2. Who were the Ptolemies and the Seleucids?

   A. _____

   B. _____

3. How did the policy of the Seleucids differ from that of the Ptolemies?

   _____

   _____

4. What does "Maccabees" mean and why was it used to describe Judas, the son of Mattathias?

_____

_____

5. Why is the BOOK OF MACCABEES important?

_____

_____

topics for discussion

1. What is your reaction to the episode described in I MC., ch.2:29 to 41? What do you think of Mattathias's decision in v.41?

2. C.S. Lewis wrote "It is great men, potential saints, not little men who become merciless fanatics. Those who are readiest to die for a cause may easily become those who are readiest to kill for it." What indications do you see in Scripture that these words were true of the Maccabees? What leaders today are examples of this statement?

3. What are some of the indications today of the tension in our country between church and state?

4. What is your opinion of people who deliberately violate laws which they consider unjust or immoral?

BACKGROUND

The Maccabees

Even as chapter 14 of FIRST MACCABEES celebrates the success of Simon and his people, a warning note is sounded: Simon is both high priest and master of the country. This will prove to be a disastrous combination. It is the foundation for the sorry and corrupt priesthood at the time of Christ. Political and ecclesiastical power can be a dangerous mixture. This Hasmonean dynasty continued until 37 B.C. when Herod the Great induced Rome to appoint him king.

The SECOND BOOK OF MACCABEES consists of letters written from the Jews of Judea to those who are living in Egypt, calling them to the unity of religious practice. In chapter 2 they call upon the example of Jeremiah urging the exiles in Babylon to observe the Lord's precepts. The story of Jeremiah hiding the ark of the covenant is recounted along with the prophet's assurance that one day it will come to light and the glory of God will be seen as his people are gathered together. This has been fulfilled in Christ, the presence of God incarnate.

Chapters 6 to 8 are also important signs of preparation for the good news of Christ. The people are again encouraged to face the suffering of persecution, but with a new reason for hope. As the tragically beautiful story of the martyrdom of the seven brothers is told, their faith looks beyond death to resurrection and eternal life. God may not miraculously rescue them from their persecutors, but he will raise them to new life.

Another belief of the Church today is reflected in the conclusion of Chapter 12 as a collection is taken up in order to offer sacrifice in Jerusalem for their fallen comrades. They offered sacrifice for the dead because belief in the resurrection had taken root among the people.

This belief is complemented by the vision of Judas Maccabees in chapter 15. As Onias the high priest prays for his people on earth, so in heaven does Jeremiah the prophet pray for them. The saints of God intercede for each other both in this world and the next. The life of God that unites them cannot be separated by death.

The way is prepared for the coming of Christ who will put the pieces together, unite all people in himself, and call us to religious observances that reflect our faith in the life of the Spirit and the resurrection and the communion of saints.

A Chronology of the Ancient World

B.C.

c. 2000	The Minoan Empire of Crete flourishing
	Appearance of the Law Code of Hammurabi of Babylon
	† Abraham leaves Ur
	† Destruction of Sodom and Gomorrah
c. 1700	The Hyksos Pharaohs reign in Egypt
	† Joseph and his brethren in Egypt
c. 1600	The rise of Athens, Thebes, Sparta, and Troy
c. 1292-25	† The Hebrews in slavery under the Rameses Pharaohs
1280	The first mutual non-aggression and defense treaty in history was signed between the Egyptian and Hittite Empires

1267	The founding of the Assyrian Empire
1220	†The Exodus of the Jews under Moses
1200-1028	†The invasion and conquest of Canaan by the Jews
1194	The Greek military expedition against Troy
1190	The Phillistines settle in Canaan
1182	Aeneas arrives in Italy
1028-1013	†Reign of King Saul
1013-973	†Reign of King David
972-932	†Reign of King Solomon and the building of the Temple
931	†Division of the Kingdom into Israel (North) and Judah (South)
880	Founding of Carthage
776	First Olympic Games
760	†Amos in Israel
753	Founding of the city of Rome
734	†Isaiah in Judah
721	†The fall of the Kingdom of Israel to the Assyrians
701	†Assyrians retreat from the gates of Jerusalem
612	Fall of Assyria before the Neo-Babylonian Empire
605	Defeat of the Egyptian army by Babylon
600	Appearance of the poems of Sappho
597	†First stage of the ˙Babylonian exile of the Jews

_____

†*Events of Sacred History*

594	Solon the celebrated legislator of Athens flourishes
586	†Destruction of Jerusalem by the Babylonian army
538	†Conquest of Babylon by Cyrus the Persian and the return of the Jewish exiles. Pythagoras, Zoroaster, and Confucius also flourished during this period.
520	†Beginning of reconstruction of the Temple at Jerusalem
509	Athens and Rome become republics
490	Darius I wages war on Greece which ends in a Persian defeat at the Battle of Marathon
458	†Return of more Jewish exiles under Nehemiah
457	Anaximander, disciple of Thales, and one of the greatest astronomers of antiquity
444	†Ezra returns to Jerusalem. Phidias, Aristophanes, and Hippocrates lived in Greece at this time.
440	Death of Herodatus the historian
433	†Nehemiah's last visit to Jerusalem
400	Trial of Socrates at Athens
348	Plato's death
335	Samaritan Temple built on Mt. Garazim
336-323	Reign of Alexander the Great
323	First partition of Alexander's world empire
322	Death of Aristotle

---

†*Events of Sacred History*

†Events of Sacred History

LESSON EIGHT

Babylonian goddess on lion
(stele from Mesopotamia)

A Guide for the Perplexed

The book we are about to study contains the fullest revelation of God's plan for man's happiness contained in the Old Testament. In a concrete fashion the author presents some of the most important themes of religion, as we shall see when we read it.

Today, when people are living out their lives in the shadow of a mushroom-shaped cloud, DANIEL is surprisingly timely. The fear of the future loomed very large in the minds of the author's contemporaries. People were tempted to compromise conviction for the sake of personal comfort or safety. They were fast losing grip on the awareness of purpose and meaning in human history as well as in their own lives. In our study we will attempt to discover how Daniel grapples with these perplexing problems of our day as well as his.

"And they celebrated the rededication of the alter for eight days": When the first excitement of the Maccabean revolt had spent itself, around 163 B.C., many of the people had second thoughts. So far the revolt had been astoundingly successful, but what did the future hold in store? They had bested a small Syrian army, little more than military police, but how would they fare against the full power of the mighty Seleucid Empire?

It may well have been at a time such as this that a now unknown Jew gathered various traditions about a certain Hebrew called Daniel who had lived through similar difficulties during the days of the Exile 400 years earlier (6th century B.C.). What God had done for Daniel, he could do again! His was a message of encouragement.

"Among them were certain Jews, Daniel, Hananiah, Mishael, and Azariah": At first we might be inclined to wonder why the author did not come right out and proclaim the ultimate triumph of God's people over the armies of Syria. Why did he choose such an indirect approach?

To answer this we must keep in mind the times in which he was writing. Israel was a more or less occupied nation. His book might be regarded by the Seleucid authorities as a pamphlet of the "resistance movement." So he chose a time in the past which paralleled his own and left clues throughout the book which his countrymen would understand.

A modern parallel to this practice occurred during the German occupation of France during the Second World War. A Paris newspaper published a poem on its front page. Read in the usual way, the poem was in praise of Germany, but if the reader divided the poem down the middle and read each half vertically, it turned out to be a condemnation of the occupation forces.

"In the first year of the Babylonian king, Baltasar, Daniel had a dream": In our Bibles, the BOOK OF DANIEL is included among the prophets. Now, although the book itself does not strictly belong to the prophetical school of writing, its position in the Bible does serve to point up an important fact. The author was not making any detailed predictions about the future, but he was writing with a truly prophetic purpose. He wanted to *proclaim* a great hope to his people and to call them to a great loyalty and watchfulness. Writing at a time when the institution of prophecy had ceased in Israel (after the Exile) he adapted the message of the prophets to the situation of his own times.

He did not intend to explain the meaning of the Exile to the people (this had been done by EZEKIEL and ISAIAH), nor to recount the history of the Return (already done in EZRA and NEHEMIAH). He did not even set himself the task of recording the events of the Syrian persecution (the BOOK OF MACCABEES had handled this). Our author dedicated his book to the task of interpreting for the people the *meaning* of this persecution. His work is unique in its insight into the essential character of tyranny, pride, the role of Satan in political tyranny, and the ultimate triumph of God. His is truly a theology of history, i.e., an explanation of historical events in the light of faith. It was his privilege to announce the supreme moment of history, the "Latter Days" and describe the realization of the "world to come," which for all its wonderful qualities is no magic world but the world *restored*.

NOW OPEN YOUR BIBLE AND READ:

The BOOK OF DANIEL, ch.1 to 7 and ch.13

behind the words

Edifying events and visions: The BOOK OF DANIEL falls into two main parts. Chapters 1 to 6, 13 and 14 contain various traditional accounts familiar to the first readers. The author has carefully selected the events with an eye to their appropriateness to the trying circumstances of his countrymen. The second half of the book, chapters 7 to 12, employs a quite different form. Here the author conveys to his readers, under the form of various visions, his magnificent theology of history for which he had prepared them in chapter 2. The various symbolic images employed were largely familiar ones, frequently found in the prophets. Each of the visions follows, more or less closely, a definite pattern. We are shown a struggle between the forces of good and evil. Then, God intervenes in a decisive triumph which brings everything to a climactic resolution. This in turn inaugurates the Divine Kingdom by a general judgment and resurrection.

WRITE IN THE MARGIN OF YOUR BIBLE:

"Daniel, his life and times"—next to DANIEL, ch.1

"The Visions of the Four Beasts"—next to DANIEL, ch.7

"The Story of Susanna"—next to DANIEL, ch.13

understanding these selections

"The third year of Jeboiakim": (DANIEL, ch.1:1) Each of the six first chapters of DANIEL is a complete event in itself. All are drawn from the period of the Babylonian exile (6th century B.C.). Four (ch.1 to 4) are set in the reign of Nebuchadnezzar; one in the time of Belteshazzar, who was governor under Naboindus, the last king of Babylon; and one in the reign of the Persian conqueror, who is here called Darius, the Mede. All six emphasize the fact that Jews were often highly placed in the pagan courts and underscore the lesson of faithfulness to God and the precriptions of the Law in the most difficult circumstances.

"The dietary laws": (DANIEL, ch.1:8) Here the author makes allusion to the practice among Jews of regarding only certain foods as proper for a Son of the Covenant. Such foods are referred to as "kosher," i.e., "clean" or "ritually pure" (LEVITICUS, ch.11 to 16 and DEUTERONOMY, ch.14:3-8). That Daniel chose what might seem to us a rather secondary point of law upon which to take issue with his pagan masters might seem strange. But to an orthodox Jew these dietary laws were an external, concrete sign of loyalty to God.

Daniel's prayer: (DANIEL, ch.2:20) This prayer is a striking testimony of the true religious outlook, gratefulness for gifts far beyond our deserts. Nothing is hidden from God and when we would have light it is to God we must humbly go.

The stone from the mountain: (DANIEL, ch.2:31-45) This vision and its interpretation gives the key to the understanding of the subsequent visions of chapters 7 through 12. It depicts the triumph of God's kingdom which is not surely just another political state but is destined as the fulfillment of the whole historical process. It is to challenge every empire and judge all policies and programs. But it is not merely an agent of judgment but also of salvation. We shall see in the Gospels that this kingdom has begun in the establishment of the Church and will reach its fulfillment in the glorious return of Christ at the "latter day." (MATTHEW, ch.28:18-20 and REVELATION, ch.22:20)

The image of gold: (DANIEL, ch.3:1) We know from many extra-biblical accounts that it was quite common among the ancients for the ruler to set up colossal images, either of some favored deity or even of themselves. In view of the period in which our author wrote (the Maccabean revolt), it is quite interesting to note that the Seleucid monarch Antiochus Epiphanes had erected a golden image of Apollo at the town of Daphne. We need not think of a solid gold statue here, but of a wooden one overlaid with beaten gold.

The handwriting on the wall: (DANIEL, ch.5) This is one of the most dramatic accounts in all of Biblical literature. It is a striking indication of the historical accuracy of even many of the details of the venerable traditions our author used. Herodotus and Xenophon, the ancient Greek historians, confirm that the city of Babylon fell by a surprise attack at night.

The lion's den: (DANIEL, ch.6:1-28) In this chapter the author speaks eloquently to such soul-searching questions as "What shall a man give in exchange for his integrity?" "To what extent is compromise ever justified?" Ancient monarchs often prided themselves on the size and variety of their private menageries, another indication of the authenticity of this and the other traditions preserved by our author.

Daniel's vision: (DANIEL, ch.7) As our author has used events from the past as a source of inspiration and encouragement to his readers, so now in the second half of the work his eye is on the future. He counsels his fellow citizens to bear up under their present trials as God is even now making ready the definitive revelation of his great plan and that soon will come the establishment of the kingdom which shall have no end. In verse 13, we find the striking reference to the "son of man" which Our Lord himself used as a reference to his second coming when speaking to the High Priest before his Crucifixion. (MT., ch.26:63-64)

Daniel the judge: (DANIEL, ch.13) It seems probable that this and the following chapter were added at a later date to the work by some unknown editor acting under the impulse of divine inspiration. They are in harmony with the general theme and purpose of the original book and probably represent other venerable traditions clustering around the name of Daniel which the editor felt should be preserved in a permanent form.

unity of the two testaments

In the vision of chapter 7, Daniel describes the appearance of "one like unto a son of man." In the BOOK OF REVELATION, (the New Testament parallel to the BOOK OF DANIEL), St. John, in his description of the Exalted Christ, makes use of the phrase, "one like unto a son of man" in obvious allusion to this passage from DANIEL. Our Lord himself frequently makes use of this messianic title in reference to his own person (MARK, ch.2:10 and 28). In fact, no other messianic title is used in the Gospels as widely. The title itself points up the position of Jesus as the representative of humanity in the great work of Redemption (EPISTLE TO THE ROMANS, ch. 5 and 8).

bible and church

The problem of how far one can go without compromising one's belief in God has plagued Christians from the time of the persecutions to the present. In our lifetime we saw how many Christians failed to stand up to Hitler and his mad schemes. Very few did, and most of those were executed. Christians face the same problem in Communist countries. Evangelicals and Jews, as well as the Orthodox, are persecuted in Russia. We have seen that priests have been killed in Poland for opposing the regime. In Central and South America, priests and nuns, along with lay people, are killed and tortured because they dare oppose the policies of those in power. The BOOK OF DANIEL offers encouragement. God's people have faced this sort of trial before, and with faith and prayer have overcome the tyrants. Therefore, we must be hopeful and confident that evil will not win in the long run.

doers of the word

The BOOK OF DANIEL was written at a time when things seemed hopeless for the Jews. It brought them a message of hope, and that message is needed in the world today. The population explosion is seen by some to threaten the ability of the world to feed its people. The threat of a nuclear holocaust hangs over our head. Revolutions and terrorists in all parts of the world threaten the lives and peace of so many people that we wonder whether this world can go on. In the face of all these threats the Christian must have hope and spread a message of hope. This message is that if we trust God and try to live up to his message revealed in Jesus Christ, things will work out to the benefit of all people. In all our conversations about the problems of the world we should introduce the note of hope based on trust in God and on an effort to live the kind of life Jesus called us to live.

questions

1. During what period in Israel's history was the BOOK OF DANIEL probably written?

2. Why is the BOOK OF DANIEL appropriately included among the prophets in our Bibles?

3. What was the purpose the author hoped to achieve with his book?

4. Why was it unwise for the author to mention contemporary events explicitly in his work?

5. How is the BOOK OF DANIEL divided?

   A. _____

   B. _____

topics for discussion

1. How do the events in the life of Daniel illustrate the place of pride in political tyranny and the brutalizing effects of absolute power?

2. What message do the events of chapter 6 have for the individual faced with a conflict between the demands of an absolute state and one's own conscience?

3. In your own life, do you feel any conflict between your faith and the demands of the government?

4. How do you respond when you hear people quoting the BOOK OF DANIEL to predict future events?

5. What benefits have you derived from studying and discussing this booklet?

6. What is the most important thing you feel you have learned from this booklet?

BACKGROUND

The Book of Daniel

We have seen a great variety of literary forms and styles in the Hebrew Scriptures; obviously they cannot all be read in the same way. In each case, the book itself gives us some clues as to how we are to interpret it. One of these clues in the BOOK OF DANIEL is the age of its hero. He begins as a young man and matures through successive reigns of pagan kings, yet he is still a young man in the story of Susanna. The always youthful hero rises to defend damsels, destroy idols, and defeat dragons. His wit and strength do not depend on natural resources, but on the wisdom and power of God.

The mode of writing is another key to the apocalyptic style. It is filled with fanciful imagery and much symbolism. This too calls the reader to transcend reality and to gain a more comprehensive perspective on time and place, a view from eternity and infinity. The author pretends to be writing in the past about future events, when in reality he is looking at the past, inviting us to see it as God sees it and to learn from this vision. This insight not only enables us to deal more confidently with the present, but empowers us to see into the future with hope. Goodness will suffer from evil in the world over and over again, but it is guaranteed that victory will rise triumphantly from what a limited vision sees as defeat. The images and symbols dramatize and heighten this conflict in such a way that people of faith in every age of the world find consolation and encouragement.

Finally, the structure of apocalyptic writing calls our attention to carefully worked literary patterns. The number of episodes in the BOOK OF DANIEL is 12 (an important symbol in itself to the Hebrews); these are divided into two sections, each of which ends in the lion pit and victorious deliverance. The first section contains three tests and three visions:

I. TEST: Daniel and companions avoid eating unclean food

II. VISION: Nebuchadnezzar's dream of a statue

III. TEST: Companions of Daniel resist idolatry

IV. VISION: Nebuchadnezzar's dream of a tree

V. VISION: Belteshazzar's dream of handwriting

VI. TEST: Daniel remains prayerful and survives the lion pit

The second section consists of four visions (two of Belteshazzar, one each of Darius and Cyrus) that are increasingly eschatological, leading to the ever-young Daniel (Israel) in Babylon rescuing Susanna (threatened innocence). Faith and prayers give him the wisdom and courage to stand up to powers of *state* in this episode, and powers of *pagan religions* in the final episode. Once again he is rescued from the lion pit, but this time it is through human mediation—a prophet, though a reluctant one. Once again, God works through people, weak and hesitant humanity, to continue the work of salvation.

Emmanuel and the Suffering Servant combine generation after generation in God's people. Jesus and the Cross lead to resurrection. The message is "good news," not to frighten or condemn but to comfort and encourage. In every age, the prophet's call to repent and believe must be echoed not only in the Word but in the Spirit of a Savior who came "not to condemn the world, but to save the world" (JOHN, ch.12:47).